GOLF

A Beginner's Guide

Jim
Doherty

Golf – A Beginner's Guide is also available in accessible formats for people with any degree of visual impairment. The large print edition and e-book (with accessibility features enabled) are available from Need2Know. Please let us know if there are any special features you require and we will do our best to accommodate your needs.

First published in Great Britain in 2012 by
Need2Know
Remus House
Coltsfoot Drive
Peterborough
PE2 9BF
Telephone 01733 898103
Fax 01733 313524
www.need2knowbooks.co.uk

Contents

Introduction

One of the most useful tools in golf for players of every skill level is self-assessment. Make that honest self-assessment. Having a clear understanding of what your goals are and what your expectations should be are two of the keys to enjoying the game of golf. We'll start this book about understanding and learning to play golf with one such assessment.

First of all, why do you want to play golf? This question is not meant to deter you. Not by any means. Rather, by taking the time to really understand why you want to play, and what you want to get out of it, will greatly improve your chances of achieving those goals, but will also determine how much enjoyment you have along the way.

People play golf for a broad range of reasons; some play for fun, others for competition, some for business, and some for social interaction, some play to get in shape, others play as substitute for activities that they can no longer play.

There's really no right answer to the question. But as you will see in the next several chapters you can take this new endeavour as far as you like. And while some may spend a lot of time, money and effort on golf, others may just have a passing fancy and only want to play a couple of rounds a year. Either way is fine and both types of players can get enjoyment from their investment as great or as little as it may be.

This book is laid out in such a way that if you are completely new to the game, you can read it from start to finish and walk away with a basic understanding of what you need to know in order to get started.

However, if you have some knowledge of the basics, this book can also be consumed a chapter at time and be used as a handy reference guide. Getting started in golf can be a bit overwhelming. In addition to having to learn how to swing a club and hit a ball (which is much harder than the pros make it look), you must also learn about which club and shot combination to use (and when), a whole set of rules, another whole set of unwritten rules and whole new language (at least it will seem that way).

Don't be discouraged. It is only difficult because most new players have to learn these things the hard way – by making mistakes in front of other people. You'll do that too from time to time as it's part of the learning process, but this informative guide will help take a lot of the initial mystery out of the game that can be a bit intimidating for newcomers.

It's also worth mentioning that most golfers (the ones worth playing with anyway) are typically patient with new golfers and willing to provide guidance and advice. So read this book and when in doubt, just ask another golfer. But be warned . . . golfers are notorious for giving each other bad advice, not out of a malicious intent, but because they did not have the advantage of a beginner's guide like this one!

Chapter information

1 – Equipment

It probably goes without saying that playing golf requires specialised equipment which, at a minimum, requires a set of clubs, a bag to carry them in and some balls (which you will probably lose on the course somewhere). At least a couple of dozen (it's better if you just accept that now!).

What you want to avoid, though, is getting all kitted out from the very start with the latest, greatest (and likely most expensive) gear. If you are not careful you can spend a small fortune on golf equipment. Once you become a proficient golfer, buying expensive clubs may be something you want to consider, but for the beginner it's usually a bad investment.

Chapter 1 covers the basic equipment you will need for both your first couple of lessons and rounds and even for your first several months as a player, should you decide to keep on with it. Before you spend a penny on equipment – be sure to read chapter 1.

2 – Golf hole features and scoring

Golf can be played on several different types of courses and if you have not been invited by someone familiar with the course you want to play, it's a really good idea to call ahead as not all courses are open to the public. This chapter discusses the different types of courses based on their access type as well as the type of holes they offer.

And speaking of holes, chapter 2 also provides a primer on the different types of holes, common features and hazards on holes, and basic scoring. We also touch on the handicap system of scoring adjustments.

3 – How to swing a club

Swinging a golf club is easy. Swinging a club and hitting a ball is hard. Making that ball go where you want it to go can take a lifetime to perfect. First though, you need to make sure you know what a basic grip is and how to make clean impact with the ball.

The chapter on how to swing a club starts out with the fundamentals – how to properly hold a club, how to position your body, how to address the ball (which is to say how to set up for a shot) and finally, how to swing a club.

It is highly recommended that you take a few lessons and spend some time on the practice range before heading out on the course. This chapter will help you familiarise yourself with what your golf teacher will cover in the first couple of lessons.

4 – Types of golf shots

There's more to a golf shot than 'grip it and rip it' – a term used to describe picking up a club and taking a big swing at a ball.

While hitting the ball a long way off a tee may seem important, it's actually a small part of the game – especially for those who want to score well. Golf is a game of precision and there are many different situations that a golfer will encounter during play that require different kinds of swings and shots.

Drives, fairway shots, shots from the rough and from sand traps, chips, lobs, pitches and putts are all 'tools' you will need to use. You may actually encounter every one of these on the first hole you ever play.

5 – How to practise

Before you play your first round it is strongly encouraged that you practise first. After your first round, assuming you want to do better, even more practice is required.

One of the nice things about golf is that once you know what you are doing, you can just go out and play. Playing on a regular basis will improve your scores, but only to a point. If you really want to get better you will need to practice. This chapter will show you how to do it the right way.

6 – Playing a hole from tee to green

Once you have learned how to swing and hit the ball with different clubs on a regular basis, you'll be ready to go out and play on the course. You'll find that in addition to the nervousness of playing with other golfers (it goes away quickly), one of the more stressful parts of playing your first round of golf is not really knowing what do when you are not hitting the ball.

This chapter walks a fictional foursome, all of different skill levels, through an entire hole from tee to green. In addition to describing the flow of the game, the chapter also provides some insight into how you can maximise your golf scores for your particular skill level.

7 – Rules and penalty shots

Despite the fact that golf is a recreational activity (and should be nothing more than that for beginners), it can also be highly competitive. As such there are many rules in the game of golf that are adhered to in varying degrees depending on the players and type of match.

Some players adhere to all of the rules all of the time. Others play a little bit loose in non-competitive rounds. Either way it's important to know and understand the more commonly observed rules of golf as well as the penalties that apply when there is an infraction.

Even if you are not competing, playing by the rules and counting your penalty strokes is the only way to accurately measure your abilities relative to other golfers. The full rules of golf are well beyond the scope of this book, but we do provide you with the basic rules and the common penalties.

8 – Golf etiquette

In addition to the written rules of golf, there is a whole set of unwritten rules and expectations of behaviour specific to the game of golf. This is probably the one area where most golfers learn only by making mistakes, which then get pointed out by a fellow golfer – sometimes by one that becomes a bit angry because of it.

Not to worry – this chapter points out some of the more common rules of golf etiquette and also provides some general guidelines that should go a long way to keeping you from making a faux pas.

9 – Golf terms

Most books offer a glossary at the end of the book to provide definitions of words and phrases that may be new to the reader.

This chapter on golf terms is at the end of the book, but it's included in the main body of the book to highlight the fact that golf has its own language that is as much a part of the game as the equipment and clothes that you need to play.

There have been whole books written on this topic alone, so this chapter will not be a complete guide. Instead we have included the terms that are either very common or are difficult to determine even in the context of playing a round of golf.

This chapter is optional, but you may wish you had read it when someone suggests you take a 'Mulligan' and you're not really sure what you should do!

Chapter One

Equipment

Before you actually get on the course, you'll need to make sure that you have the proper equipment. There is a long list of equipment that you could buy, and if you are not careful the price can add up very quickly. In fact, golfers spend well over ($20 billion) £12.3 billion every year on equipment alone according to the National Golf Foundation (NGF.org), an industry association that tracks worldwide golf participation and spending.

This chapter will provide you with a list of the bare essentials that you need to play your first few rounds of golf and then expand to cover the equipment you may want consider if you decide that you enjoy the game and want to continue on a regular basis.

Equipment for your first few rounds

For your very first round of golf you will only need a few basic items. These items include a bag and a set of clubs, some golf balls, a handful of golf tees and a golf glove.

For your first few rounds of golf you may want to borrow or rent clubs rather than investing in a starter set of clubs, as it is the least expensive option. Keep in mind though that golfers can be very touchy about their equipment, especially given the cost of a high-end set of clubs that have been custom fitted. It's considered bad form to ask to borrow another person's main set of clubs, particularly if they play on a regular basis. A better (more polite) way to approach the subject is to ask if they have an old set of clubs that you can borrow. Most people who have an old set of clubs will more than happy to loan them to you. In fact, they may even ask if you are interested in buying them, which, depending on the price and condition of the clubs, can be an affordable way to get your first golf set.

'For your very first round of golf you will only need a few basic items.'

Something else worth mentioning here, and this could very well go in the chapter on etiquette, but it fits better here: if you borrow a friend's bag and clubs do not use that person's golf balls. Golf balls are not that cheap (especially the high-end brand name balls) and as a beginner you are likely to lose a lot of them. You can probably use some of their golf tees in a pitch but the polite thing to do is buy your own consumable items. Remember that your friend did you a favour by letting you use their clubs. Don't take advantage of them, and if you ever want to borrow them again, make sure you clean them before giving them back.

If you don't know any other golfers, or if the ones you do know don't have a spare set you can use, renting a set of clubs is another good option. If you are planning on renting clubs from the course where you are playing it's best to call ahead of time to see if they even offer rental clubs (not all courses will have this option). If they do not, the local golf or sporting goods store may have a rental option as well.

For everything else you need you are better off going to a sports shop or a department store (one that has a sporting goods section). You can purchase all the items that you will need, but most pro shops (the ones at the course) cater to avid golfers and carry only the high-end brands, which almost always cost more.

Golf balls

You will want to buy at least a couple of sleeves of golf balls (they come in small boxes of three) or a box with a dozen. Come to think of it, you should buy two boxes of a dozen. You are much better off as a beginner having a greater number of less expensive balls, than having fewer more expensive balls because you are likely going to need them. Ignore the marketing on the box. Instead grab the least expensive balls the shop has to offer because, regardless of what the top brands claim, you are not going to hit those balls any further, truer, sweeter, or more reliably than the box of cheap balls you could and should be buying. A lot of these ball are going to be lost in the woods or hit into lakes and you'll feel a lot better about it knowing that you mitigated your losses by going with the less expensive balls.

Tees

Another item you will want to buy is a large bag of tees. The cheap ones are fine. Again don't fall for marketing gimmicks. The job of the tee is to hold the ball up in the air to make it easier to hit off the tee box. It's a pretty simple job and the plain old wooden tees do it well.

Golf gloves

Another item that's worth having is a golf glove. This may seem unnecessary but the glove will not only help you grip the clubs, but it will also help prevent blisters. Your first time playing will likely result in you swinging the club over 300 times, accounting for the driving range, your practice swings and the actual swings at the ball. If your hands are not properly conditioned (and maybe even if they are) you could end up with some nasty blisters that could cause a lot of pain and discomfort.

When shopping for a glove you will want to get one that fits snugly, but not too tightly. The glove will go on the hand that is closer to the (intended) direction of travel of the ball. For right-handed golfers this is your left hand, and for left-handed golfers the glove will go on your right hand.

What to wear

As far as apparel for your first time out – wear comfortable, loose-fitting clothing that allows you to move without restriction. Given that a round of golf can last up to four hours, it's a good idea to check the weather forecast for the whole day (rather than just sticking your head out of the window right before heading to the course). The weather and temperate can vary considerably from the beginning to the end of a round of golf, and it can make for a long day if you get caught on the course unprepared. Remember too, that some golf courses have a dress code and if you show up wearing jeans and T-shirt you may not get to play. It's always a good idea to ask before heading out.

'The job of the tee is to hold the ball up in the air to make it easier to hit off the tee box. It's a pretty simple job and the plain old wooden tees do it well.'

Footwear

For footwear you will want to wear running shoes or some other comfortable shoes with good treads (to keep your feet from sliding around). Sports shoes with spikes or moulds, other than golf shoes, are not allowed and should not be worn as they can seriously damage the putting greens.

Stick to the basics

There are dozens, perhaps even hundreds, of different items you can get beyond this basic list. Some of them will probably be useful if you start to play on a regular basis. However, most of them are really only designed to separate you from your money. For any gadget or device you see that you may want to get here's a good rule of thumb – don't buy any item (beyond the basics) until you have played three rounds where you could have actually used the item in question.

'Used clubs are a good option if price is your main consideration.'

Equipment considerations if you decide to keep playing

If, after the first few rounds, you decide that you 'have the bug' and want to keep playing, you will want to consider getting your own clubs. There are a lot of options from used to new and if going for new clubs, the options cascade from there.

4 Iron   6 Iron   9 Iron

Loft comparison of irons

Pre-owned clubs

Used clubs are a good option if price is your main consideration. Go to any online auction website and there will be hundreds of used clubs you can purchase. This is a good way to get a full set of clubs and you may even get a high-end set (perhaps one that is just a couple of years old) for a decent price. The main downside to this is that you are limited to what is available on the second-hand market, and while the price might seem like a good deal, the clubs you are getting may not be what's best for your game. If your goal is to play on a regular basis, with the idea of learning the finer points of the game and improving your score, a used set of clubs is probably not the best option for you. If, on the other hand, you just want a decent set of clubs to go out and have fun with once in a while, this is a really good and affordable option.

If you do want to improve your game though, getting the right set of clubs is an important consideration. A word of caution though, there is no replacement for a good golf swing and there is no club that will correct a flawed swing, so make sure you work on your golf swing. That said, there are certain types of clubs that are made specifically for beginners. Forget what the pros are using, and for the most part forget what your friends are using, especially ones who are good golfers. Having a very good and consistent swing allows golfers to use clubs that have a better ball action, but they require that the ball be hit correctly and have less room for errors. You can spend the money on these clubs but they won't work as well for you and in fact they may actually hurt your game rather than improve it.

For beginners

For beginners you are better off getting a set of 'beginners' or 'game improvement' clubs. There is no shame in these designations – it's more about getting the right tools for the job. Generally speaking, beginner's and game improvement clubs are perimeter weighted (you may also hear the term 'cavity backed') and have a greater loft on a per club basis than standard or high-end clubs.

Shifting the weight of a club to the back and rear of the club guides the swing into a more natural arc, which helps the golfer develop better swing mechanics. A higher loft will sacrifice distance for height, which is fine for beginners, since getting the ball up and out after making contact will be a bit of a struggle at first. At this point in your game you are much better off getting the ball up in the air, and the first time you hit a 'pretty golf shot' you will likely be hooked for good.

Hybrid clubs

Another common component of the beginner's set is the wide use of hybrid clubs which combine the distance of a fairway wood (3, 4 and 5 woods) with relative ease of the mid and long irons (irons 2-5). These clubs come in very handy when you are off the tee box but still have a long way to go to reach the green. They are also easier to hit than a driver and many players use them off the tee box as well. Hybrids are so easy to hit that most players (and even some pros) carry at least one in their bag.

3 wood (left) as compared to a hyrid (right)

Number of clubs

Another consideration for your first set of clubs is the number of clubs in the set. While the maximum number of clubs a player can have in their bag is fourteen, as a beginner you will actually need far fewer clubs to start with. This is one of the nice things about a starter set – fewer clubs means less money. To start with you probably only need a driver, a hybrid, two to three mid irons, and pitching wedge, a putter and maybe a sand wedge.

Customising clubs

Once you've decided on a set of clubs, you may want to get them fitted. There are going to be some limitations on the amount of customisation you can to have done to a beginner's set, and you will probably not need custom shafts or any other add-ons. However, if you are shorter or taller than average you will want to get your clubs made to the right size.

Putters

The final consideration for clubs is the putter. You can spend a fortune on a putter if you are not careful. The best thing to do (assuming that your starter clubs do not come with a putter) is to try a few inexpensive putters in the store. Putting is about feel, so if you are going to buy a putter try two or three out in the store. A better option is to borrow one or two and try them out on the course. This will not be possible if you order online or go to a sports shop, but most traditional golf shops will let you borrow a putter to make sure it's right for you before you commit to a purchase.

Other odds and ends

If your starter set does not come with a bag then you will have to get one to carry your clubs around in. There are a number of options and, like all things in golf, there is a huge price range among the various options. Two features that you'll want to look for are: a double shoulder harness and a fold out bag stand. These are common features on most golf bags today.

The double shoulder harness allows for a balanced weight distribution as you carry your clubs around the course. Your golf bag might not seem that heavy (even with the clubs and balls in it) but by the 18th hole it may feel like a sack of bricks. The double harness is better for your back as well.

A fold-out bag stand is an attachment to your bag that allows it to free stand when you set it down. Not only does this keep the bag cleaner by keeping it off the ground, but it also makes it easier to set down and pick up, and makes removing and replacing your clubs before and after shots a lot easier.

Summing Up

- When you first start playing golf, only buy what you need, i.e. the basic equipment – golf balls, a golf glove, a set of clubs, tees and a bag.

- Try before you buy – see if you can borrow an old set of clubs from a friend whilst you try your hand at this new game.

- Keep initial costs down by investing in second-hand equipment; you can always purchase more expensive, higher-end gear as you progress in the sport.

- Spend wisely, don't be fooled into buying equipment you don't need. Remember, the equipment you do buy will not make you shoot par – only investing in lots of practice and effort will help you do this.

Chapter Two

Golf Hole Features and Scoring

With an understanding of the equipment you will need to play golf, the next step is to learn a thing or two about golf courses, golf holes and scoring.

This chapter starts out with a review of the different types of golf courses and the different types of golf holes and their features. We end the chapter with an overview of scoring and how golf handicaps work throughout the game.

Golf courses

Golf courses can be categorised by the number and type of holes. A standard golf course has 18 holes with a mix of par 3, par 4 and par 5 holes that total 36 per nine holes and 72 for the entire 18. 'Par' means the 'expected' score by proficient players (very few golfers actually achieve par for the whole round) and the object is to score at par (or lower) for each hole and/or the round. The three types of holes, par and the scoring adjustments to even out playing abilities (called handicap) are discussed in the following sections.

In addition to the standard 18 holes some courses only have 9 holes that players play twice to complete a standard round. Other courses have more than 18 holes. Some of these have distinct sets of 18-hole courses and some allow players to mix and match different pairings of 9 hole sections to make up a standard round.

Par 3 courses are made up of entirely (or mostly) par three holes. Executive courses are much shorter courses designed for fast play. Approach courses, while rare, are great courses to practise the short game, which are the shorter shots used to get the ball on the green and putting.

'A standard golf course has 18 holes with a mix of par 3, par 4 and par 5 holes that total 36 per nine holes and 72 for the entire 18.'

Types of golf courses

Many people consider golf to be an exclusive activity but that's not really the case. While there are some private clubs that have exclusive membership and limited access there are also many courses that are open to the general public – including some very fine golf courses that are even used in professional tournaments. The section below describes golf courses based on their access.

Public courses: Public golf courses are open to the general public who are required only to pay 'greens fees' for each round played. Players are usually required to call ahead to schedule a tee time but in some cases players will tee off based on a first come, first served basis. Possibly one of the most famous (and oldest) courses available to the public is St. Andrews Links, which has hosted 28 British Opens to date.

Private courses: The classic view of the country club is the private course. Private courses require players to pay a membership fee and in some cases there is both an initial fee and on-going membership dues. The fee amounts can vary considerably, from modest fees, to extremely high fees, which of course exclude all but the wealthy. Many private clubs require new applicants to be nominated by a current member. One of the most famous exclusive clubs in the world is Augusta National, which is home of the Masters Tournament. Augusta National has only 300 members which include some of the richest and most powerful people in the world. Private clubs usually allow non-members to play as guests of members, although non-members are almost always required to pay greens fees.

Semi-private courses: Semi-private courses allow non-members to schedule a tee time and play the course (without being invited by a member) but they also sell memberships to players. Members of semi-private courses will typically be given access to desirable tee times before non-members and will usually get a better price per round average if they play more than a couple of times per month.

Resort courses: Resort courses are typically packaged as 'Destination vacations' where golf is included as part of a resort package. Guests of the resort are given preferred tee times and discounted feeds.

Golf hole features and hazards.

As mentioned previously, a standard golf course has 18 holes that includes a combination of hole rates as par 3, par 4 and par 5 with the total adding up to 36 on the first 9 holes (called the front nine) and the 36 on the last 9 holes (called the back nine) for a total of 72. Most standard courses will have a pair of par 3s and a pair of par 5s on both the front and back nine. Standard courses are usually between 6,000 to 7,000 yards long for the entire course (the total of all holes from tee to green).

Golf holes

Golf holes have a number of features on them, some of which are on all holes in the same relative position, some of which are on most holes in different positions and some which appear intermittently from hole to hole. The common features are discussed below.

Tee box – The tees box is the area from which golfers take their first shot on every hole. There can be more than one tee box on a hole, which are used by different golfers and in different situations. For example, there is usually a tee box set further away from the green that is used for tournaments. The tee box is a well-manicured section that is often elevated slightly. On the tee box players are allowed to place their ball on an elevated tee to make it easier to hit.

Fairway – The fairway is the main part of the hole leading to the putting green. In the fairway the grass is kept shorter and the surface is well maintained. The fairway is often kept narrow (relatively speaking) to reward players who can control their shots, as it is easier to hit a ball from the shorter grass. All but the shortest par 3 holes (which players are expected to reach the green in a single shot from the tee box) will have a fairway.

The rough – Adjacent to the fairway is a section of longer grass called the rough. The ball is hittable and playable from the rough, but the longer grass impedes the swing making the ball a bit harder to hit and affecting the distance and accuracy of the ball.

'Hazards are usually strategically placed to force players (especially good players) into risk-reward decisions.'

The deep rough – Some holes will have what is referred to as the deep rough. This area is typically an unkept natural area that, while still in bounds, is very difficult to hit from due to uneven ground and obstructions such as trees, roots and shrubs.

Out of bounds – Some holes will have a boundary marked by white stakes that the player cannot play out of. A player hitting a ball out of bounds must re-hit from the original location and the player also incurs a penalty stroke. (Penalty shots are discussed in a later chapter.)

The fringe – This is an area that surrounds the green. The fringe is usually about 3 yards with slightly longer grass than the green. Players can either chip, pitch or putt from the fringe.

Putting green – The final section of the hole is the putting green which includes the cup, which is the objective of the hole. The cup is marked by a flagstick that can be seen at a distance.

Hazards

Hazards are obstructions placed on the course that players must avoid or traverse in order to reach the green. There are two types of hazards and each has two classifications. Each is discussed below.

- Water hazards are naturally occurring or manmade bodies of water that are permanent features of a golf course. There are two types of water hazards. A standard water hazard (which is just called a water hazard) is a water feature that is usually placed in such as way that the golfer must hit over the water in order to reach the green. A lateral hazard is water that runs parallel to the hole that the player must avoid but is not generally required to hit over. There are different rules for where to re-hit from if your ball goes into a water hazard but both result in a penalty.

- Bunkers or sand traps are depressions filled with sand. Sand traps are also qualified based on their location. Fairway bunkers are bunkers that are not near the green, but they do not actually have to be in the fairway. Green side bunkers are usually placed adjacent to the green as the name suggests. Hitting a ball into a bunker does not incur a penalty, but they can be difficult to hit out of.

Hazards are usually strategically placed to force players (especially good players) into risk-reward decisions. For example, a hazard may be placed at a distance that would put a player in an excellent position to get a low score on a hole but would require a very good (long and accurate) shot. Failure to hit such a shot would probably result in a penalty shot which of course would lead to a higher (less desirable) score than what the player would have probably achieved by playing safe.

Types of holes

As mentioned previously, holes are rated on a par system that denotes the number of strokes it 'should' take a player to get from the tee to the cup. The par system assumes that a player will take two putts to hole the ball once they have reached the green and the term 'being on the green in regulation' accounts for this. For example, on a par three you would need to hit your tee shot onto the green to be 'on in regulation'. This does not mean that you cannot 'par a hole' if you are not on in regulation, nor does it mean that you will score par if you are (for example you could three putt).

What should be obvious though is that par 3 holes tend to have relatively short distances from the tee to the green and par 5 holes tend to have very large distances between the tee and the green, the distance does vary.

'Holes are rated on a par system that denotes the number of strokes it "should" take a player to get from the tee to the cup.'

The following illustrations show the diagrams for each type of hole and several of the key features are pointed out as well.

Hole #2 Yardage
Par 3 - 197 165 145

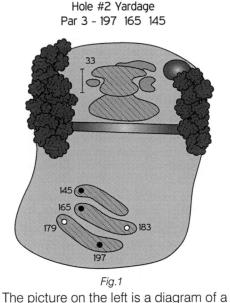

Fig.1

Blue Ash Golf Course
Hole #3 Yardage
Par 4 - 391 375 276

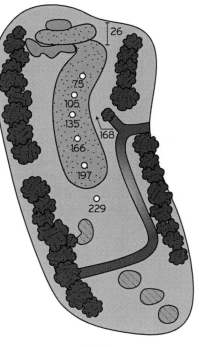

Fig.2

The picture on the left is a diagram of a par 3 hole. The numbers shown after the par rating are the yardages from the three main tee boxes (from longest to shortest are the tournament tees, the men's tees and the women's tees) which are shown on the diagram.

Note that this hole has a water hazard and three green side bunkers. The lighter shaded and dotted section with the vertical stripes depicts the fairway (which is smaller on a par three hole). Also shown is the green (the diagonal striped section) which shows the distance from front to back.

A diagram like this is often shown on the score card or on a sign near the tee box. While the diagrams will vary from course to course in detail and quality, most will show the basic features.

Blue Ash Golf Course
Hole #5 Yardage
Par 5 - 514 496 419

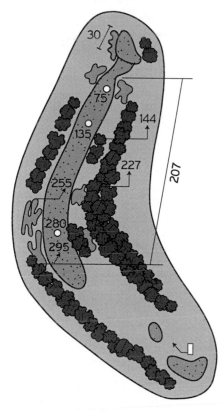

Fig.3

The diagram to the right of the par 3 hole shows a par four. Note again the yardages shown which are longer than that of the par three in the previous diagram.

An interesting feature of this hole is that the stream running through the hole is both a water hazard from the back tees and a lateral hazard from the front tees and fairway.

The white dots with the numbers note the distance from that location to the centre of the green. You can usually see the distances marked on top of sprinkler heads through the fairway. This helps golfers determine what club to use.

The final diagram above shows the features of a par 5 hole. Note the longer distances from tee to green.

The hole also has a turn in it, which is referred to as a dog-leg. In this case the hole is a dog-leg right because it turns to the right.

This hole also features a number of fairway bunkers that must be negotiated. For a better player this would require a well-placed first shot in order to avoid the hazards.

Scoring

As indicated before, the object of golf is to get the ball from tee to green and in the cup in as few strokes as possible. Each hole (and by extension the whole course) is rated which allows players to compare their scores against both par and other players. There are additional designations from par that help players understand their scores relative to the par. This helps players distinguish between scoring a 4 on a par five, versus scoring a 4 on a par three. From top to bottom the hierarchy is as follows:

Hole in one – As the name suggests, this is when a player puts the ball in the cup directly from their tee shot. When this happens (and it's quite rare) it's almost always done on par threes where the greens are usually reachable in one shot

Double eagle – A double eagle occurs when a player scores three under par on a hole. When it happens it would always be on a par five, because three under on a par four would be a hole in one. The double eagle is statistically rarer (and some people feel it is more impressive) than a hole in one because it requires two nearly perfect back-to-back shots over a long distance.

Eagle – An eagle is a score that is two under par.

Birdie – A birdie is one under par.

Bogey – Bogey is one over par.

Double and **triple bogeys** are two and three over par respectively.

Some of these can be extended to an entire round as well. For example, playing bogey golf means the player averages one over par on every hole and therefore 18 over par for the round.

Handicaps

Because golfers of different skills often play together, and in some cases compete against each other, a handicap system has been developed to level the playing field between golfers of different skill levels.

During handicap play, a weaker player is given a stroke on certain holes, depending on their handicap. The formula for computing a player's handicap is actually quite complicated as key ratings of the courses played are taken into account beyond the player's score. Fortunately, most courses will have an automated system that calculates the the player's handicap.

Scores, however, are used in calculating a player's handicap – the system uses the best 10 scores from a player's last 20 rounds to create a kind of running average. A player who is improving will slowly reduce their handicap. Players who shoot par or better will not require a handicap and are referred to as 'scratch players'.

Handicaps do sometimes cause controversy because they are used in tournaments to adjust scores. Some players use the system to their advantage by recording rounds with either scores that they actually achieved, or by playing at a level that is less than their skill to drive their handicap up. During a tournament they would play better than their handicap but still receive the adjustment.

For example, a played who is skilled enough to be a five handicap player could record twenty rounds leading up to a tournament that averaged eight over par. This would drive their handicap to an eight (this is not exact but for the sake of illustration it's passable). During a handicapped tournament they would play to their ability (five over par) but they would still get the 8-stroke handicap giving them a net score of three under par. This practice is called 'sandbagging' and is highly frowned upon.

As a beginner you probably won't need to worry about calculating your handicap, but it does help to understand basically how it works. You may get asked, 'What is your handicap?' and it's perfectly acceptable to say you don't have one, or that you are a 'high handicapper'.

'As a beginner you probably won't need to worry about calculating your handicap, but it does help to understand basically how it works.'

Summing Up

- Par means the number of shots and putts it should take to get from the tee to the hole, and the total of those shots and putts for an entire course. Therefore, it implies the 'expected' score for proficient players per hole, per round.

- The object of golf is to score at par (or lower) for each hole or the round. (Very few players actually achieve par for the round.)

- There are a number of hazards found on a golf course, designed to affect gameplay and test players' skill levels.

- The handicap system allows players of different skills to compete on a level playing field.

Chapter Three

Swinging and Hitting

Millions of pounds are spent every year by golfers on clubs, balls and gadgets all promising to fix golf swings or compensate for less than perfect golf swings. The sad reality is that most of this is just wasted money. If you fail to learn how to swing a golf club in a way that allows you to consistently hit the ball squarely with the clubface, you will not score very well in golf. (Note that there was nothing in that statement about a 'perfect swing' because any swing that moves the club low and through the ball with the club head striking the ball square and clean at the point of impact is a good one.)

That said, it has been shown over time that in order to achieve consistent results swinging a club, you will need to grip the club properly (and there is more than one way to do this), address (or set up to) the ball in a way that allows you to take a full swing while maintaining your balance, and then swing at (and then hit the ball) in a synchronised manner.

If you have attempted to swing a club and hit a ball, you will see that it's not as easy as the pros make it look. Not even close. However, after a little bit of instruction and some practice you will get the hang of it. They key to a good golf swing is to learn how to do it correctly from the start, because if there is one thing harder than learning how to develop a good swing it's unlearning a bad one.

'The key to a good swing begins before you even address the ball.'

Getting a grip

The key to a good swing begins before you even address the ball. Having a proper (and consistent) golf grip on the club is critical to striking the ball properly so it's worth doing right. There are different types of standard golf grips and while every grip is unique to each golfer, a good golf grip will have some elements that should be adhered to.

In addition to helping your hands get in the right position at the moment of impact (which in turn squares the face of the club), a good golf grip will also help transfer power from your hips, back, shoulders and arms to maximise the power of your swing. This does not mean you have to swing hard – in fact it's the opposite in that a good grip will ensure that that maximum amount of power is transferred from your swing which allows you to swing in a controlled manner, while still imparting a great deal of force to the ball.

Grip types

- The ten-finger grip – With the ten-finger grip the player wraps all ten fingers around the club. This grip is most often used by children, people with small hands and athletes from other 'stick sports' who are more comfortable holding the club this way based on their experience. Most golfers will move away from this grip over time.

- The overlap grip – With the overlap grip the player places the pinky finger of their right hand in over the groove between the index and second fingers of the left hand (for a right-handed golfer). This grip is most often used by professionals.

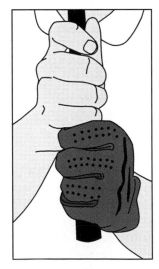

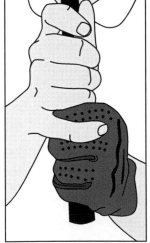

Ten-finger grip	*Interlock grip*	*Overlap grip*

Need2Know

- The interlocking grip – The interlocking grip is variant of the overlap grip where the pinky finger of the right hand hooks the groove and the index finger of the left hand (again this assumes a right-handed golfer). Many golfers use this grip for putting even if they use the overlap grip for their swings.

With all grips the thumbs overlap so that the right thumb is on top of the left thumb (opposite for left-handed golfers) with both thumbs pointing down the shaft of the club.

One of the first things you will cover in your first lesson, if you decide to take lessons, is the golf grip. Your instructor may recommend that you use the overlap grip, which most people find awkward at first. It's worth sticking with it though because it has been shown to be the best performing grip, and eventually it will become comfortable for you.

Addressing the ball

Now that you know how to grip the club you need to set up for your shot. This is commonly referred to as 'addressing the ball'. Like the grip, the set-up for the shot is a very important aspect of being in position to strike the ball squarely and cleanly at the bottom of the swing.

When setting up to hit the ball your body is positioned parallel to the target line of the ball.

Balance is a critical aspect of a golf swing and you will want to have your weight on the balls of your feet and evenly distributed – eventually you will shift your balance slightly depending on the club, but for now a 50/50 weight distribution between is the way to go.

Getting into position

Knees should be bent slightly and the hips should be dropped and pushed slightly towards the back (rather than bending at the waist) – this is a subtle but important distinction and it should be practised.

Your arms should hang naturally, and in the correct position your hands will be about level with the zipper of your trousers.

'When setting up to hit the ball your body is positioned parallel to the target line of the ball.'

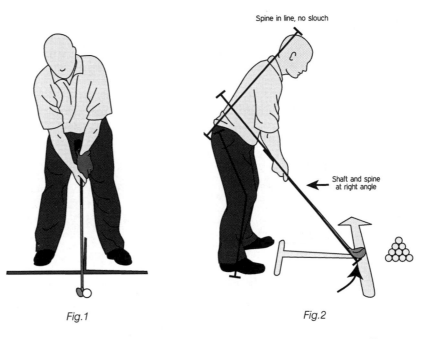

Spine in line, no slouch

Shaft and spine at right angle

Fig.1   Fig.2

The ball should fall close to the middle of your stance, although this will vary depending on the club (with shorter clubs you want the ball further back in your stance).

Prior to initiating your backswing you will want your upper body to be tension free – this is not always easy, especially when you get nervous. A good tool for pre-swing tension release is to squeeze all of your muscles right after setting up, hold the tension for a moment, and then release it. This tends to work because it makes you aware of all of the tension (especially through the back and shoulders). It's easier to let the tension go once you are aware of it.

This set-up will feel very awkward at first but it's important to get it right. One tool that is enormously helpful is video. This used to be a very expensive add-on option to private lessons but now you can do it for free with most smart phones. It's one thing to hear about what's not quite right with your swing but it's another thing entirely to see it. Have a friend take a video of your swing and then ask the instructor to critique the swing while you are both looking at it – this will greatly shorten the process of learning a proper set-up (and swing).

Backswing

Once you are set up, your backswing begins – you'll begin to move the club back, keeping your lead arm straight in a smooth and steady motion. When your hands are about waist high your hips will start to slightly rotate away from the ball. Your wrists will begin to cock as well.

When your swing is about three quarters of the way through the swing the shaft of the club will be almost vertical and the club head will be well above your head. Your weight will have begun to shift to your back leg (the leg away from the target).

When you are at the top of your backswing your weight will have shifted mostly to your back leg but you should still have good balance. The motion of your arm should have turned and raised your target side shoulder under your chin.

At the top of your backswing you should be wound up like a spring – however your target side eye should still be on the ball. Remember that if you can't see the ball, you can't hit it.

Once the top of the backswing is reached you will immediately begin your downswing – there should be no hesitation at the top.

The swing is initiated with the hips beginning to turn back to square and the lead arm coming back through the backswing path.

One thing to note – and this is something most beginners get wrong – you do not want to swing down or chop at the ball. Rather, you want to bring the club head around in a wide arc so that the club head is low and sweeping through the ball at the point of contact.

When your lead arm is again about waist high your wrists are still cocked. As you begin to square your hips your wrist should be breaking to increase the club head speed as it comes low and through. At the point of impact you should be square with the ball and slightly behind it, with your weight shifting to your front leg. You should be looking at the ball through this entire sequence.

After impact you will continue your swing all the way through until your hips are roughly square to the target. Your front leg will remain in place, but your back leg, by necessity, will be bent. Most of your weight will be on your front leg at the completion of the swing.

Summing Up

- Swinging to hit a ball correctly is by no means as easy as the professionals make it look, and takes a considerable amount of practice to perfect.

- There are three common methods of gripping a club: the ten-finger grip, the overlap grip and the interlocking grip.

- Having a good grip, addressing the ball correctly and standing in a good position are all key elements of an effective golf swing.

- Enlisting the help of a qualified golf instructor is the best way to learn to 'swing and hit'.

Chapter Four

Golf Shots

Just as important as the clubs in your bag, are the shots you make with them. In fact, many golf instructors would argue that learning and then gaining some level of mastery of the basic golf shots is far more important than the clubs you make them with. Sure, there are specially designed clubs for almost every golf shot, but until you learn how to make each shot with confidence, no club, no matter how specialised, is going to help you out.

This chapter covers the basic golf shots you should know in some level of detail. What the shot is, when and where it's used, and tips are all covered. These shot types include tee shots, hitting irons off the ground, chipping, pitching, lobs, bunker shots and putts. We'll also cover some not so common shots at a summary level that you can work on after you get the basics down.

Tee shots

At the start of every hole golfers tee up a ball on the tee box to hit their drive. Unless you are on a par three hole, or if the design of the hole dictates otherwise, most players will use a driver (1 wood) or some other wood to maximise the distance off the tee. Even for avid golfers, hitting off the tee can be a nerve-racking experience, especially on the first tee when there are several groups of golfers waiting to tee off and everyone is watching. Here are some key things you can do though to help maximise the effectiveness of your drive.

First of all, remember the real purpose of the tee shot or drive – the purpose of the tee shot is *not* to see how far you can hit the ball! The real purpose of the drive is simply this – get the ball off the tee and into play to set up your next shot. Preferably on the fairway, but, at a minimum, in a playable lie. That's it. The drive is not about distance and this is the biggest mistake that most golfers make.

'Remember the real purpose of the tee shot or drive – get the ball off the tee and into play to set up your next shot.'

The fact is that unless you are an exceptionally good golfer, trying to muscle a drive (or any other shot) to maximise distance is a recipe for disaster. Even professionals hit shots into the woods on occasion when they try to squeeze out a few more yards on a shot.

The most important thing to remember about a golf swing is that strength has almost nothing to do with hitting a golf shot – control and precision and striking the ball cleanly – are far more important; trying to hit the ball hard makes a clean strike next to impossible.

Driving off the tee

So how do you apply this? For beginner golfers the best advice is don't hit a driver off the tee box until you are very comfortable with that club. Remember that there is a rule that says you have to hit a driver on the tee box, and chances are that a higher number wood such as a 3, 4 or 5 wood is much easier to hit. You can even use a hybrid wood, which for many players is even easier to hit than a 5 wood. Using a non-driver also helps you reinforce the idea that you are not going for distance off the tee. The purpose of the tee shot is to get your ball in play. Ignore the good golfer that you are playing with who rips one 280 yards down the fairway. For you (and for most players) a 100-yard shot that leaves you in play is vastly superior than a 190-yard shot that goes into the woods.

You will want to eventually be able to use your driver off the tee though, because a longer drive is better, assuming that you can hit a control shot. The problem is that most people (especially men) get their driver out and then go into 'smash' mode. One of the issues is that when you practise on the driving range the hitting field is very wide to accommodate a lot of hitters, but it gives you a false sense of hitting in play. When you practise hitting with your driver (and you will see in the chapter on practice that you should do this less often than you think) try to hit your ball inside of some boundaries on the range (these can be real or imaginary). Once you can do this on a reliable basis then you are ready to try it on the course.

But always remember – 100 yards of the tee in play is a much better shot than 200 yards into the woods.

Fairway shots

Once the ball is in play you'll need to hit the next shot off the ground, which, depending on the lie, can be bit more difficult to hit than hitting off the tee where the ball is elevated and you are on flat surface.

Just as you do from the tee box, you have the option of using several clubs depending on the nature of the shot and situation. If you are still too far from the green to get there in a single shot, your best option is probably a hybrid club which is easier to hit than a fairway wood, and again the idea is to move the ball forward while keeping it in play.

If you can reach the green in one shot – but are not yet hitting an approach shot, as defined on page 40, you'll be hitting with a mid-range iron. This is where some practice on the range can pay off. After several practice sessions with your irons you should have a pretty good idea how far each of your clubs will carry when you hit a good shot. As a beginner you are probably not going to hit a good shot every time, but it's still a good idea to pick the right tool for the job.

The same rule above about drivers applies here. Nobody is going to care if you can hit a 6 iron 80 yards rather than 60 yards. Know the distance of each club and use the right tool for the job. Generally speaking, as the distance of a club goes down, the accuracy should go up – for example, an 8 iron will go a much shorter distance than a 4 iron, but you should be much more accurate with the 8 iron.

Hitting from the rough

Hitting from the rough is a bit different from hitting from the fairway because unlike the neatly trimmed fairway, the grass in the rough will impact both your swing and the ball as it comes off the club. In this section we are talking about the standard rough – the somewhat taller grass that flanks the fairway.

When hitting from the rough you will usually want to use one club more than you would normally hit from that distance because the longer grass will slow down the club speed as the club head sweeps through the grass at the bottom of the swing. The term 'one more club' means you use a lower number club – which of course is counter-intuitive as clubbing up or clubbing down refers to distance – which is opposite of the club numbers, where the lower the number of the club, the longer the distance you will hit it. For example, if you have a shot from the rough that is from a distance where you would normally hit a 6 iron, you will want to hit a 5 iron.

Remember, when hitting from the rough following through on the swing is very important. If the grass is very thick this will be harder to do so remind yourself as you set up, to follow through on the ball. This does not mean you want to swing harder – just club up, take a normal swing and commit to the follow through.

Odd lies

'When hitting from an uphill or downhill lie, match your shoulders to the slope when addressing the ball and take a nice easy swing that allows you to keep your balance.'

Another shot that you will encounter is the uphill or downhill lie. Many beginner golfers get thrown off by these lies because they have only practised their swings on a flat surface. Once they get out on the course they are faced with slopes and hills and they are not sure what to do. There are many articles and even several books dedicated to these types of shots, but for the beginner here's all you need to remember. When hitting from an uphill or downhill lie, match your shoulders to the slope when addressing the ball and take a nice easy swing that allows you to keep your balance. Also, remember that the slope of the hill will add or detract to the loft of the club. On an uphill lie you will get more loft – so club up. On a down hill lie you will have less loft, so club down.

If at all possible, practise hitting from uphill and down hill lies. More and more modern courses have an abundance of rolling hills and other features, so having some experience with these shots before they come up during a round will save you some stokes.

Approach shots

When it comes to scoring in golf, mastery of the short game (which results in greater accuracy) is the most important aspect. This makes sense in that a golfer who can make accurate approach shots that result in short putts (meaning they can hole out in one putt) will have many fewer strokes per round than a player who has to two putt once they are on the green (assuming relatively equal putting skills which evens out for most players for anything beyond a 10 foot putt).

Need2Know

Think about that – being accurate on your approach shot can drop your score about 8-12 strokes per game. That's a huge improvement! The key to improving is practice, practice, practice; and the chapter on practice is mostly dedicated to the short game (hopefully you are seeing a pattern here). First though, let's define the approach shots.

Chip shots

A chip shot is a low, short shot that rolls after landing. Chips shots work much the same as long putts, but in this case you are using an iron, taking a very abbreviated backswing and then following through on the ball. The length of the total distance will determine the club speed, but remember that with chip shots most of the distance the ball travels should be on the ground rolling. Chip shots are usually taken with a specialised iron or a mid-short iron such as a 7 iron. When chipping you want to pay attention to the breaks in the green since the ball will be rolling a great distance. Keep in mind that breaks in the green have greater impact at the end of the chip or long putt when the speed of the ball slows.

Pitch shots

A pitch shot is used when you want the ball to carry some distance, but not move much after landing. Most golf sets come with a pitching wedge with a lot of loft. This not only gets the ball up in the air, but aids in imparting a backspin on the balls which counteracts the forward momentum of the ball in impact with the ground. Key to a good backspin is follow through, which brings us to an important point about hitting with a pitching wedge.

At some point on a golf hole you will be inside the range of your shortest club, which means you can no longer club down. This is classic pitching wedge territory and you will need to learn to hit three quarter and half swing shots to shorten the distance of your shortest club. Many beginners think that hitting a short shot requires a shorter swing but this is only half right (which means it's also half wrong). The key to hitting shorter shots is to take an abbreviated backswing, but still fully follow through. This is critically important when pitching, because it's the best way to drop the ball in close and have it stop once it lands (or at least keep it from rolling off the back side of the green).

'When it comes to scoring in golf, mastery of the short game (which results in greater accuracy) is the most important aspect.'

If you are really interested in playing good golf, the short game is where you should focus most of your time and energy. One of the best references ever written on this topic is *The Short Game Bible* by Dave Pelz. In it Dave mathematically proves that the short game is the primary determinant of scoring in golf and then provides a wealth of information on how to practise and improve your short game.

Bunker shots

Beginner golfers learn all to soon that green side bunkers are a lot easier to get into than then they are to get out of.

'With a little practice and an understanding of how to hit a shot from the sand you will be able to swing with confidence and get out of bunkers reliably.'

However, with a little practice and an understanding of how to hit a shot from the sand you will be able to swing with confidence and get out of bunkers reliably. With more practice you can get to the point where you get out of the bunker and close to the hole.

As odd as it may seem, the key to getting your ball out of the bunker is to not hit the ball. This does not mean you pick your ball up and throw it (it's tempting though!). What you want to do for a bunker shot is swing the club *into* the sand starting about two to three inches behind the ball and then follow through completely. Swinging the club into and through the sand forces the sand into the ball, which lifts the ball up and out of the bunker.

This is something that requires practice to get right, not just because of the mechanics required but also the psychological aspects of the shot. One of the hardest things to get your head around with a bunker shot is that you have to commit to the swing but you also have to commit to the sand. Doing one and not the other can cause problems. For example, if you hit behind the ball (into the sand) but don't follow through (and it's hard to, so this is the one place on the course where giving the swing some 'oomph' is a good idea) you'll only end up a foot ahead of where you were – with the ball still in the sand. On the other hand, if you commit to the swing, but fail to drive the club head into the sand behind the ball you will pick the ball out clean and end up hitting the ball well beyond where you want it to go.

One thing to note on a sand shot. On most shots you can set the club head on the ground when addressing the ball. This is called 'grounding the club'. When you are hitting from a hazard (including both water hazards and bunkers) it is illegal to ground your club, and doing so will cost you a stroke. As a beginner it is doubtful that you will get called on this, but it's best to learn how to set up a sand shot correctly since it's such a common part of the game.

Putting

Putting is a topic all to itself. This chapter does not cover putting in great detail as it is beyond the scope of this book, but we would be remiss if we did not mention it here. The key to putting is to have a good, smooth, consistent putting stroke.

Green speeds and breaks in the green will obviously impact a putt, so it's critically important to practise as much as you can. When putting you want to try to stroke the ball hard enough so that a missed putt (one that is offline) goes past the cup by about one or two feet. Remember the putt that is short has zero chance of going in so if you are going to miss, miss long.

'The key to putting is to have a good, smooth, consistent putting stroke.'

Other shots

Two other common shots that you may hear about are 'lay ups' and 'punch' shots.

A lay up shot is when you intentionally club down to avoid a hazard or trouble. For example. If you have to hit over a water hazard and the carry of the shot (the distance from where you are to where the ball would first strike the ground) is too long, or would require a perfect shot, which is low percentage for most, you may want to consider taking a much shorter shot that will make the next shot easier.

A punch shot is used when there are overhead obstructions, such as tree limbs that would probably affect the ball if you were to hit a normal golf shot. Punch shots (or knock downs) are also used when hitting into the wind where keeping the ball low will lessen the effects of the wind. The more common application of this shot for beginners is to get the ball back in play after hitting a shot into the woods. This is a shot you can ask an instructor to help you with after you have become proficient at the other swings.

Summing Up

■ Mastering the basic golf shots is one of the most important elements of the game.

■ Every game starts with a tee shot. It's important to remember this shot is not about distance (as many golfers mistakenly believe), but about precision (aiming to keep the ball in play).

■ Getting out of a bunker is a lot harder than getting in to it! But with practice and an understanding of sand shots, you will be able to get out of bunkers capably.

■ The key to putting is a smooth, consistent stroke – again learned with practice.

Chapter Five

Practice

If you are like most golfers, there's a very good chance that you are not going to be very good at it in the beginning. Even players with natural ability still don't tend to play very well, at least not initially. The best way to fix this of course, is to play more, and to practise. Playing more golf is pretty obvious, but if you want to accelerate your improvement you need to practise and most people simply don't practise in a productive manner.

This chapter will provide some practice tips that will help you get the most out of practice to ensure that the time you spend practising leads to lower scores.

Hire a pro

While there are a lot of things that you can learn by watching a YouTube video, a proper golf swing is not one of them. There is really no substitute for having a registered professional instructor show you how to swing different types of clubs for different types of shots. Considering that a series of lessons (even as few as three to four sessions) will cost only a fraction of what the latest greatest clubs would, you are better off buying a reasonably priced set of clubs, paying for a few lessons and pocketing the difference. No matter what the marketing brochures tell you, no club will fix a bad swing.

If you do hire a pro, be very specific about what you want to accomplish. Tell them you are a beginner golfer and would like a few lessons on how to hold and swing a club, and how to hit the various shots including driving, fairway irons, chipping/pitching and putting, with a strong emphasis on the last two (more on this later).

Practise more on the shots that count

Go to most practice areas on a golf course or to your local driving range and you'll typically see that most of the golfers are on the driving range rather than the putting green, and most of those golfers are hitting balls with a driver or wood. This is simply backwards.

While it is important to learn how to hit a good drive, the amount of time and emphasis placed on this shot is radically disproportionate to the number of times that particular shot is taken on the course and the overall importance of that shot with regards to the score that golfer achieves. What this really boils down to is most men (this is largely a male issue) want to impress their buddies by hitting the ball further off the tee than the other golfers they are playing with. While this may be satisfying to the ego, hitting the ball long off the tee has been statistically proven to have almost nothing to do with scoring well in golf. In fact, trying to hit the ball long off the tee is one of the biggest higher (worse) scores in golf because the ball is more likely to go out of bounds or end up in the deep rough, both of which add strokes. Most golfers, and especially beginners, are much better served by focusing more on hitting the ball cleanly and keeping it 'in play' off the tee than they are trying to out hit their mates.

'From a practice standpoint you will want to allocate about the same percentage of your overall practice time that your drives or tee shots make up in your game.'

From a practice standpoint you will want to allocate about the same percentage of your overall practice time that your drives or tee shots make up in your game. On a typical golf course you will use your driver (or other wood such as a 3 wood) 14 times, because there are usually four par three holes on a course where, due to the shorter distance, you will hit a mid-range or short-range iron off the tee box. For a beginner golfer assume that you will be somewhere in the 90s or higher, so you should probably be spending no more than 20% of your practice time on hitting a ball off a tee, and the focus of that time should be on hitting shots that stay in play.

The rest of your time should be spent on mid-range shots, trouble shots and short game with a strong emphasis on the short game

Mid-range practice

Mid-range practice consists of your 2 iron through to your 9 iron and can include hybrid clubs as well which are relatively new clubs in the game of golf which give wood-like distances from a club that swings like an iron (which are generally easier to swing). Accuracy – not distance – is one of the most important aspects of golf and when you practise with your irons you want to focus on first determining your accuracy and then working to improve upon it.

Something that will be very productive for you as a beginner golfer is to spend some time on the range determining the distance and accuracy with each of your clubs. Neither of these will be great to begin with but you want to strive for consistency. The best way to do this is to hit a couple of dozen balls with each of these clubs, or at least the ones you are going to be using the most. Hitting a 2 iron or 3 iron is difficult for avid golfers so leave those in the bag (if you even have them). However the irons 4-9 (or the ones you have in that range) should all be practised with.

When practising with these clubs you will want to remember to take the same swing with each of them – remember that there are different clubs for different situations and it's usually a mistake to try and swing harder at a ball with a one club when a more controlled swing with a higher number club would have gone the same distance. When practising, hit a couple of dozen balls with each club (you do not have to do every club in a single session), and using the yardage markers or flags try to determine the distance that each club averaged on the shots where you struck the ball well. You'll hit a lot of bad shots, but don't worry about those. Once you determine the rough distance of the club, pick a target on the range and try to get close to it on every practice swing. Remember that when you practise – you should be focused on improving your accuracy, of which distance is only a single component.

'Something that will be very productive for you as a beginner golfer is to spend some time on the range determining the distance and accuracy with each of your clubs.'

Trouble shot practice

This is probably the one area of golf where everyone should practise more, even good golfers. Practising on the driving range is all well and good, but you can probably count the number of times on one hand where you hit a shot on the course where both your feet and the ball are on a level surface and the ball has an ideal lie. Far more common are shots from bad lies, inclines, declines, deep rough and rough ground. This is especially the case when you are beginning.

Here's why it's so important though to practise these shots. One of the keys to scoring well in golf is to minimise mistakes. This includes both wasted shots, where the ball either goes nowhere or ends up in a worse position, and shots that end up in penalty strokes. As you begin to play more it can be an eye-opening experience to keep track of wasted shots. It's a good bet that the number subtracted from your score would have resulted in a very respectable round. They say the aim is not to play every shot perfectly, but rather to minimise big mistakes.

That said, hitting from trouble shots or from situations that get players into trouble is a major component of golf, and one of the things that makes it both interesting and challenging. Practising these shots can make a huge impact in getting out of trouble cleanly or avoiding it all together.

It's not always easy to practise these shots and most driving ranges will not be set up to accommodate this type of practice. Many golf courses, however, will have some practice areas set aside for this, allowing players to practise bunker shots and other shots from less than ideal lies. If you have access to a club ask the club personnel if there are practice areas that allow for different types of sites. If they do not have this, a good way to practise is to go on the course when it's not that busy and hit several shots from different lies and approaches.

You'll want to get permission from the pro shop to do this, but if you want to improve your scores this is one of the best areas for improvement. You can also use this type of practice as you improve. The pros spend a great deal of time mastering every shot from every situation – beginners and even avid amateurs would do well to imitate them as their time allows.

Short game

If you want to score well and become a good golfer, the majority of your practice time should be spent on your short game. The short game includes chipping, pitching and other approach shots (the shot that gets you from the fairway to the green) and putting. More than any other part of the game, a proficient short game is the key to scoring well in golf, and improving one's short game will have an immediate and obvious impact on your average score.

As with the mid-range irons, accuracy is the key to your short irons which includes the 9 iron, pitching wedge, lob wedge and sand wedge. You should also practise pitching, which often involves an abbreviated swing, with a 7 or 8 iron to achieve a short shot of 10 feet that rolls after landing.

For longer chips or lobs, the practice range is a good place to get some work in. On most ranges there will be flags set up at short and intermediate distance. It's worth the time to spend an entire session at the range with each one of your short clubs to get a feel for and improve upon, your accuracy with each shot. As much as accuracy is important with the mid irons, accuracy is critical in the short game where the difference between a three foot putt left from a chip and nine foot putt could account for an extra stroke or two on the putting green.

For the shorter chips and pitches it is acceptable to use the practice green that is usually placed in proximity to the driving range. You'll want to be sure you can control your swing to the point where you can hit soft shots that will not endanger anyone else using the practice green, or if need be, wait until the green is clear so that you can practise these critical shots

If you do get a series of lessons, the primary focus of the lessons, after getting the basic swing mechanics down, should be on the short game. Practice, practice, practice. While your friends are on the driving range trying to knock the dimples off of range balls you can be actively improving your score by chipping balls onto the putting green trying to consistently leave the ball within a makeable putt.

Putting

Assuming you can swing a club and reasonably move the ball from tee to green, putting is the area on the course that is most associated with low scores. In fact it's so linked to scores that many golfers track putts separately (and in addition to) their total score as a measure of how they played. Most golfers will want to average two putts or less on every green. In fact, the term 'being on the green in regulation' refers to getting the ball on the green with two stokes remaining to make par. This may be difficult to achieve for a beginner golfer but the idea of trying to average two putts per green is a game within the game and is a good goal even for beginners.

Obviously, this is greatly impacted by the accuracy of your approach shots. If you can consistently get the ball to within six feet of the cup on your approach (not an easy task) you have a great chance of meeting or exceeding that goal. However, whether or not you can become that accurate you will still need to develop a consistent putting stoke and become proficient at reading breaks in the greens and adjusting your aim to account for them. The only way to do this is to practise. Be warned, there are many gadgets out there that claim they can help you – golf devices is a multi-million pound industry all by itself, and while some are slightly more effective than others (and some are just plain wastes of money) there is no substitute for getting on a real green and putting a ball.

Summing Up

- The best way to learn about the game, and how to play it, is to enlist the help of a professional/instructor. A series of lessons will help you perfect your swing and understand the various types of shots and when to use them, and what clubs to use for them.

- Practise shots that really count in your game. For example, don't be tempted to spend too much time on the driving range practising your drives, as these do not make up a large proportion of your game.

- It's important to concentrate on improving your short game, for example approach shots, chipping and putting, so the majority of your practice time should be spent on this.

- Make sure practice is productive – always have a specific area of focus and improvement for your sessions. Remember – don't just practise, practise with purpose.

Chapter Six

Playing From Tee to Green

If you have never played golf before it's probably a good bet that you are nervous. Not only because you have to try and hit that tiny ball on the ground, but also because you don't really know what to do. This chapter will walk you through play on a typical golf hole with a group of four players.

To make things a little easier we are going to give names to our group and use a set of diagrams to walk you through the hole. Our four players will be Bob, a low handicap player; Tom, a high handicap guy who is decent but who tries to play beyond his skills and does not practise much; Alice, a female player who is a mid-handicapper; and our beginner, Jim, who is on the first hole of his first round. This hole happens to be a par 4 hole.

Who goes first and where do you hit from?

Golf is a game of etiquette and there are procedures for the order of hitting. First, however, let's figure out where to hit from. On most golf courses there will be several sets of coloured markers or signs that designate different types of tees. Starting from furthest away from the green are the 'Back tees' or 'Championship Tees'. In some cases there will be a second tee placed for professional tournaments, these are often marked black or white and referred to as the 'tips'.

White tee markers are usually referred to as 'tournament' or 'challenge' tees. Again, these are reserved for low handicap players or as the name suggests, for tournaments.

Yellow tee markers are typically referred to as 'Men's tees' and are used in most players. Red tee markers are referred to as 'Ladies' tees'.

The tees are usually well forward of the men's tees and if there is a hazard set in front of the tee box that has to be hit over (such as a water hazard) the ladies' tees are often placed on the far side of the hazard. The red tee positions are designed to even out the biggest difference between men and women players of equal skill, namely the distance they hit the ball off the tee box. However, you will find that good female golfers will hit from the white tees, and it's OK for men (especially for beginners) to hit from the red tees. Most men won't do this even if they are beginners but if you can set your ego aside it's really a good idea to hit from the red tees, especially if hitting from the white requires hitting the ball over a hazard (why waste a ball?).

As far as the order goes, there are some general rules, as well as some practical considerations. If your group has a player who plays the round from a different set of tees – for example, if you are playing with people who are using the ladies' tees, if the tee box is more than a few yards ahead of where the rest of the group is hitting from, those players hitting from the back tees will hit first and then the whole group will move to the forward tees to allow the golfer(s) using that tee to hit their shot(s). This is done for both safety and efficiency.

Outside of that consideration, the order of hitting the tee shot is based on what is called 'honours'. Honours dictate that order of teeing off is based on the scores from the previous hole, where the best (lowest) score from the previous hole gets to hit first, followed by the second lowest score.

On the first tee the order can be determined by a coin toss, or by tossing a tee in the air and the player it points to once it lands goes first. The group can also just pick a random or not so random order.

As far as where to hit from, the ball can be placed anywhere between the markers, bounded by the line the markers form and as far back as two club lengths. Hitting ahead of the tee markers will incur a penalty in tournament play.

Starting play

Getting back to our foursome from before, the three men flip a coin and by coincidence they tee off in order of their skill, with Bob, the best golfer in the foursome, going first. Jim ignores the advice and hits from the men's tees.

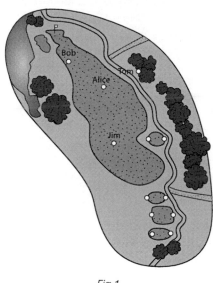

Fig.1

Bob hits a very good shot, which travels nearly three hundred yards and ends up on the left side of the fairway, leaving him in good shape to get on the green with his next shot.

Tom then tees off, and despite the fact that he's not nearly as good as Bob, and does not play as often, he foolishly tries to match Bob's drive. The result is a ball that goes far, but ends up in a cluster of trees in the right rough.

Jim, the beginner, goes next, and while he does not hit the ball very far he at least makes contact and the ball gets about even with the ladies' tees where he should have started from anyway.

The group then walks up to the ladies' tees where Alice hits. She hits a nice shot which does not go very far compared to Bob and Tom, but she lays it up right in the middle of the fairway.

At this point everyone has teed off and all 'lie 1'. The ball positions are shown in Figure 1.

Since Jim is furthest from the hole or 'away' in golf speak, it's his turn to hit again. Bob suggests that he use a hybrid club. It's the right club but Jim swings too hard and tops the first attempt, causing the ball to pop up and roll about twenty feet. Bob suggests he slows down a bit and just focuses on making contact with the ball. Bob reminds Jim that, as a beginner, chances are he's not going reach the green on this shot no matter what, so the best plan is

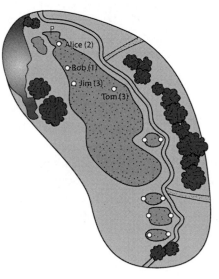

Fig.2

to move the ball forward and keep it in play. Jim takes his advice and hits a pretty good shot. It's low to the ground, but once it stops rolling, his ball is almost even with Bob's ball.

While Tom is looking for his ball, Alice takes her shot. It's a nice shot that lands on the front edge of the green. After Tom finds his ball he sees that he has a difficult shot to make through a couple of trees. Bob suggests that he play it safe and just chip it back to the fairway. That would cost a stroke, but then he has a nice approach shot to the green. Tom says he thinks he can reach the green from where he is.

It's a surprise to no one but Tom that his ball ricochets off a tree and ends up even deeper in the rough. Tom now acquiesces and uses his pitching wedge to hit a soft shot perpendicular to the hole to get back on the fairway, not far from where Jim's ball is. This is called 'getting back in play'. Tom now lies 3, meaning he has taken three shots to get to where he is. Figure 2 shows the location of everyone's balls and the total number of strokes that everyone has taken.

Tom now takes his fourth shot and the ball lands on the far end of the green. After two more shots he is on the fringe of the green close to Alice. Bob hits a pretty second shot about six feet from the pin.

On the green

With everyone now on (or close to) the green the bags are placed off to the side of the hole. Bob and Alice grab their putters while Tom and Jim both grab a putter and wedge. Bob marks his ball since he is close to the pin where the other players will be hitting. The ball positions are shown in Figure 3.

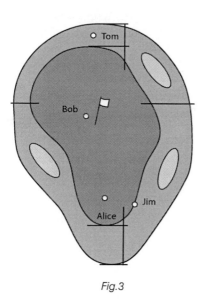

Fig.3

Tom is away and he tries to pitch the ball to the green to get it to roll towards the pin. He puts a little too much on it and rolls the ball about 10 feet past the cup. He marks his ball and steps to the side. For Jim's turn, Alice suggests that he putt even through he is on the fringe. This is allowed she tells him and it's an easier shot to control. Since Jim is putting, and Bob and the others are on the green, Bob removes the pin and places it off to the side. Jim takes Alice's advice and while his aim looks OK, he leaves the ball about 9 feet short.

Alice then putts and she leaves the ball about five feet short.

Tom is now away so he putts again. He rolls a nice putt up to about 8 inches from the cup. As he walks up to his putt Bob says, 'You're good' and Tom picks up his ball. This is referred to as a 'gimmie' which means that the making of the next putt is a virtual certainty, so the player who has been given a gimmie picks up the ball on the assumption that his next putt would have gone in. Tom ends up with a 7 on the hole.

Jim's next putt rolls two feet past the cup, but on his next putt he holes the ball.

Bob now replaces his ball and squats down about 6 feet behind the ball to read the green, which means he is trying to determine how the ball will break once he putts it. Many players will do this, and sometimes from more than one angle. This is OK too, as long there is not a group coming up from behind you or if you are in a tournament. Generally speaking, you should be reading the green while other players are putting, so long as you can do this without interfering with their shot or causing a distraction. Bob makes the right read and sinks a nice putt.

Alice then takes her putt, which is on line, but circles around the rim of the cup and ends right on the edge of the cup without going in. This is of course a 'gimmie' but she walks up and taps it in.

Counting it all up

Bob, the best golfer in the group, ends up with a 3 on the hole. This is one under par, which is called a 'birdie'. Bob is a good golfer and did what good golfers do – he was on the green in regulation (meaning he left himself two putts to make par) and then he made a nice putt. With a lot of practice you may get to play like Bob some day, but it does take dedication.

Alice ends up with a 5 on the hole, which is one over par, or a 'bogey'. She nearly made par but missed a close putt. Interesting here is that Alice does not hit the ball very far, but she manages to stay out of trouble. This conservative approach is what most golfers should emulate as you can manage pretty decent golf scores just by not making big mistakes. You may not get a lot of birdies like Bob, but you'll avoid disaster holes.

Tom ends up with a 7 on the hole or 'triple bogey'. This is not a great score for an experienced golfer and you've seen that Tom can actually hit the ball pretty well, so what exactly happened? Tom's first mistake was that he tried to match Bob's drive. The problem with this is that Bob is a much better player than Tom and Tom should be focusing on his own game and his actual abilities. His attempt to hit the ball as far as he could resulted in his ball going into the woods. On his next shot, once again, Tom tried to hit a shot that he was not capable of hitting. Instead of just taking the safe shot he tried to make a very low percentage shot and he was lucky the ball did not go out of bounds, which would have cost him two more strokes. Once he got back in play he did pretty well. In fact, if you eliminate his mistake he saves one stroke for sure and maybe two. The lesson here is don't try to play beyond yourself (which happens more often when you play with a good golfer), and don't try to fix one mistake by making another one. Golf has a tendency to punish bad decisions. Alice played a much more conservative hole and she walked away from it a lot happier than Tom did, who tried to play beyond his ability.

Jim's ends up with an 8. Not terrible by any means for his first hole, and only one higher than Tom who plays a lot and hits the ball much further than Jim can right now. Jim's objective on the hole was to try to make good contact with the ball (which he did a couple of times) and to try his best to move the ball down the hole and keep it in play. He accomplished all three and he can leave the hole feeling pretty good about how he played.

Summing Up

- Golf is a game of etiquette and procedures – from the beginning, knowing where to tee off from, knowing what order to tee off in on each hole, through to putting, maybe declaring if a player has a 'gimmie'.

- As the example game in this chapter showed, the conservative approach to each hole and shot is best, instead of trying to play beyond your abilities.

Chapter Seven

Rules and Penalty Shots

A game of rules

Golf is a game steeped in rules, protocols and traditions. In fact, the official *Rules of Golf* is nearly 200 pages long, and a violation of a rule, or assessment of a penalty, typically results in a penalty stroke (or two) and in some cases may result in the loss of a hole or a match depending on the type of round being played.

While this may seem a bit intimidating to the beginner golfer, many of the rules will not apply outside of tournament play and you will find that in many cases, even avid golfers do not have a full grasp of all the rules.

This chapter on the rules of golf will explain some of the more common rules that apply in everyday golf, and which ones you can probably let slide in a friendly match.

It's worth mentioning though, that in a tournament, handicap round or friendly wager game, the rules of golf should apply – and it's expected that players police themselves. As a beginner you are better off avoiding 'competitive' play, but knowing the rules and playing by them will make you a welcome addition to a group and will help you get an accurate assessment of what your capabilities are.

'Golf is a game steeped in rules, protocols and traditions.'

Rules that apply in all rounds

Playing the wrong ball

While this may seem obvious, you should never hit or move a ball that is not your own. In a tournament this could result in the loss of a hole, and in handicap play it will cost you a penalty stroke. However, even outside of that, it can really annoy somebody and is best to be avoided.

The actual rule states that if a player plays the wrong ball they are assessed with a one-stroke penalty *and* that the player must continue to use that same ball for the duration of the hole. At the completion of the hole the player can revert back to their own ball.

Many players will use a permanent marker to put dots or other marks on their own ball to help identify it on the course, since there's a good chance of another player using the same type of ball.

If you happen to hit your ball into another fairway it's usually OK to keep playing your ball and try to hit it back onto the hole you intended to play, but be careful not to walk into another player's swing. Also, remember that if you happen upon a ball that does not belong to you or a member of your group – it may be someone else's errant shot and it's best to leave it alone.

Lost ball

If you cannot find your ball during play it's acceptable to look for the ball and others in your group may help you look for it. About five minutes is the maximum amount of time you should spend looking for your ball, less if there is a group behind you waiting to play.

If, after looking for your ball, you cannot find it, you must declare a lost ball. In a tournament or in handicap play the *Rules of Golf* state the you must take a two-stroke penalty and go back to the approximate location of where you hit your last shot from, and play a new ball from that location again.

In a friendly game it's usually acceptable to take your two-stroke penalty and drop the ball where you thought your ball should have been, assuming it was in play. When you are just starting out, don't worry too much about the penalty strokes (assuming it's a friendly game).

To take a drop you must stand straight up, extend your arm fully (to the front or side) with your arm parallel to the ground and drop the ball without exerting influence on it. In others words you can't spin or direct the ball in any way. Just drop it and play it where it lies.

Unplayable lie

An unplayable lie is a situation where it's not possible to hit the ball with club. For example if your ball ends up wedged under the root of a tree that is in bounds, you have an unplayable lie. Example: if you had taken your second shot and it resulted in an unplayable lie you would remove your ball from the unplayable location and drop it in a playable area within two club lengths – you take a one-stroke penalty and are now hitting your fourth shot.

For unplayable lies you are assessed a one-stroke penalty and must drop your ball within two club lengths from where you picked up, but no closer to the hole. You may also go back to where you originally hit the ball and hit again from that location. From the example above if your second shot resulted in an unplayable lie, you could pick up your ball, go back to where you hit that shot from, drop the ball and you would now be taking your third shot. Use discretion with this option – if you have people behind you it's better to take the penalty shot and press on.

'For unplayable lies you are assessed a one-stroke penalty and must drop your ball within two club lengths from where you picked up, but no closer to the hole.'

Removing debris and touching the ball

This is one of the more loosely interpreted rules during golf, from friendly rounds to handicap rounds, and often causes players to lose strokes in tournaments because of a lack of understanding.

A ball on the course (not including the green which has its own rules) must be played where it lies and not be touched other than the act of taking a swing at the ball. This even includes removing loose debris around the ball. This can be done, but the rule states that if the ball moves while you are removing debris (sticks, leaves, dead birds, whatever) you are assessed a one-stroke penalty.

The same goes for touching the ball with your club while addressing the ball – it counts as a stroke if you touch it.

However – many clubs have what they call 'winter rules' which when posted gives players the leeway to improve their lie. In other words, the presence of winter rules does away with the penalty stroke for touching the ball by specifically allowing you to move your ball a few inches here or there (with your hand, the club or even your foot) with the specific purpose of making it easier to hit your next shot.

For beginners it's generally accepted that you will play winter rules but many players get so used to moving their ball to improve their lie on the course they simply forget that this rule even exists. Keep this rule in mind as you play – it's good practice to 'play it where it lies' as often as you can.

The two exceptions to this rule are when the ball:

- Is obscured by a manmade object such as a yardage marker, buggy or other objects.
- Lands on 'ground under repair' which should be clearly marked with a sign.

In both cases you are allowed a 'free drop'.

Out of bounds (also called 'OB')

During play you will notice a series of white stakes on the edge of some holes – typically these are on a tree line or at the borders of the course (although they can be on the interior as well)

These white stakes mark the out of bounds line for a hole. Hitting a ball outside of the imaginary lines that connect the white stakes results in a one-stroke penalty and requires that you re-hit your ball from the original location.

If you hit a shot that you believe may have gone out of bounds, you can declare that you would like to take a provisional shot (or just a 'provisional'). Here's how a provisional works.

Provisional

After hitting the provisional, you go to look for your original shot. If the original ball is in bounds, you play that ball without a penalty – just pick up the ball you hit as a provisional. If that was your first shot (your tee shot) you would now be hitting your second shot.

If the original ball was out of bounds you must pick that ball up and play your provisional shot from where it now lies. If, as in the case previously, your tee shot (the first shot of a hole) was the one that went out of bounds. You would be hitting your fourth shot.

This last part is a point of confusion – many people see this as a two-stroke penalty. Here's how it adds up. Your original shot goes out of bounds – you hit that shot so it counts as a stroke. You are then assessed a one-stroke penalty. You must now re-hit from the original location – that is your third stroke (and this is the shot you are taking when you take a provisional). Your next shot – assuming that it's in play, is your fourth shot.

Water hazards - hitting the ball into the water

Golf course designers (most of whom are evil by nature) place obstacles throughout the course to make your day miserable and cost you lots of money in lost golf balls. One of their favorites tools is the water hazard. For most beginners these lakes, ponds and streams will seem like ball magnets. You'll want to be familiar with the penalties.

Hitting your ball into the water hazard will cause you one-stroke penalty, but there are two types of water hazards that determine where you get to drop the ball.

The nastier of the two hazards is a water hazard marked by yellow stakes. These hazards are intentionally placed between the player and the green. If you hit a ball into water you are assessd a one-stroke penalty and you must drop your ball on the same side of the water hazard that you took the shot from. In other words – the rules force you to attempt to hit your ball over the water again. For example, if your tee shot (first shot) goes into the water, you are supposed to hit your next shot from the same side of the water. You would be taking your third shot.

'Hitting your ball into the water hazard will cause you one-stroke penalty'

For beginners it's usually OK to drop your ball on the far side of the water to avoid losing a fortune in golf balls, and it's also OK during friendly play to hit a ball you don't mind losing and then switch balls once you are clear of the hazard (remember though that the actual rules state that you must play the same ball for an entire hole if it remains in play).

The second type of water hazard is a lateral hazard. A lateral hazard is water that is not in the direct path of the hole – for example, a stream or pond that is off to the side of a hole. Lateral hazards are marked with red stakes. If your ball goes into a lateral hazard you are assessed a one-stroke penalty and must drop the ball within two club lengths of where the ball went into the hazard, but no closer to the hole.

There is also something called 'casual water'. This is water that is not supposed to be on the course. For example, if a large puddle forms on the course after heavy rain. If your ball lands in casual water you are allowed 'relief' which means you can move your ball and drop it on normal ground without a penalty.

Other rules you should know about (but usually don't apply in casual play)

The following few rules are included here because the situations they apply to tend to come up fairly often during a round of golf. Most of the time the rules below are ignored but it's important to understand them. Many players have been surprised by these rules when it counts, so it's best to understand them even if they do get ignored during casual play.

Too many clubs in the bag

The rules state that the maximum number of clubs in a bag is fourteen. A player can be assessed a two-stroke penalty for every hole they have played with more than fourteen clubs in their bag.

Asking another player about their club selection

Asking another player what club they are playing will result in a two-stroke penalty – this is a rarely enforced rule but it's worth knowing about. You can look in another player's bag to see which clubs are still in there without penalty, but if that player has placed a towel or some other cover on their bag to obscure this, you are not allowed to move it – doing so results in the same penalty as asking.

Hitting the flagstick with a putt

When putting you are not allowed to hit the flagstick – it should either be removed, or if you need to use it as a guide, you should ask another player to attend it. Attending the flagstick means a member of your group, or a caddie, holds the flagstick while you are putting. Once the ball is in motion the person attending removes the flagstick from the cup. If a player putts into the flagstick they are assessed a two-stroke penalty.

Putting into another player's ball

If you are on the putting green and you putt the ball into another player's ball (which is also on the green) you are assessed a two-stroke penalty. The player who was not putting can place their ball back where it was. The player who was putting must play the ball where it lies.

You are allowed to mark your ball if it is in line with another's putt or in a position where a missed putt will potentially hit the ball. How to properly mark a ball is covered in the chapter on etiquette.

'Asking another player what club they are playing will result in a two-stroke penalty – this is a rarely enforced rule but it's worth knowing about.'

Recording an incorrect scorecard

In a tournament if a player signs a scorecard with an incorrect lower score they are disqualified. This has actually happened in PGA tournaments and the players have lost several hundreds of thousands of dollars/pounds as a result.

Summing Up

- As a beginner, it is not essential to adhere to all of the rules all of the time, but understanding and following the most common rules will give you a better assessment of your ability, and you can establish an accurate handicap.

- In a tournament, all of the rules must be followed unless otherwise noted by a tournament official.

- If you plan on playing on a regular basis you should familiarise yourself with the official *Rules of Golf* book so you don't run into any surprises when you find yourself in an official round that requires strict adherence to all the rules.

Chapter Eight

Golf Etiquette

A game of customs and courtesy

In addition to the rules noted in chapter seven that have to do with scoring and competitive aspects of the game, there are many rules of behaviour and courtesies that should also be observed.

It's a good idea to familiarise yourself with these rules and, as in any new situation, it's a good idea to watch and do what others do (most of the time). As with the rules, if you are unsure about something to do with golf etiquette, just ask.

Remember that etiquette always applies, even in non-competitive matches, and it's especially important when you are the guest at another person's club. Misbehaving may not only get you kicked out, but it could also impact your friend's standing.

Respect the course

Obey the course signs and rules

This should be obvious, but if there is a sign telling you to either do something, or not do something – follow it. This can include signs that make sense, such as 'no carts/buggies beyond this point' and other signs that may not be as obvious.

Signs such as '90-degree rule in effect' are signs you will see from time to time. The 90-degree rule means that a buggy or cart must stay on the cart path until you are even with the ball, at which point you turn 90 degrees and drive to where your ball is. After taking the shot you drive directly back to the path and proceed towards the green on the cart path. You do not need to follow this rule

'Remember that etiquette always applies, even in non-competitive matches, and it's especially important when you are the guest at another person's club.'

to the letter as it may create a dangerous situation (if there is a sharp drop off from the path or if you are adjacent to a hazard you are allowed to modify the angle a bit. The point of the 90-degree rule is to keep the buggies off the course as much as possible.

If there is a sign that reading 'cart path only' or 'buggy path only' it means buggies and carts (the motorised ones that you ride in) must stay on the path. In this case you are to drive the cart up to where the ball is and then walk from the cart path to the ball. It's good practice to take a couple of clubs if the ball is more than a few yards away and you are unsure of what type of shot you must hit.

If there is no such sign you can drive the buggy over the course, however never drive the buggy onto the approach, the green or in a sand trap (bunker).

Keep time

Keeping time in golf is important to both the course and the other players on the course. While you don't have to be rushed, it is expected that you show up to your scheduled tee time and that you keep pace on the course.

On most courses you will be assigned a tee time at the clubhouse. If you are just showing up (as opposed to being invited by someone) it's a good idea to call ahead to reserve a tee time for a group or to ask for a tee time. You are expected to be on the starting tee (almost always the tee box for the hole number one), 10 minutes prior to your starting time. On some courses there will be a starter to let each group know when they should begin. It's a good idea to know what order you will tee off in prior to your start.

If there is no starter ask the pro shop for the name of the group ahead of you (they will probably tell you anyway). Upon arriving at the first tee, simply ask the people standing there which group or party they are with. Once the group has hit and are out of the range of your group's first shots you may then begin to hit.

Be quiet

Golf is a social game and it's perfectly acceptable to carry on conversation with members of your group and at times it's acceptable to be a bit loud. However, it is expected that everyone should remain quiet while a player is hitting and putting. If you are in the middle of a conversation you should pause while a person is addressing the ball or setting up for a shot and remain quiet until they have completed their stroke.

You should *always* turn your mobile phone off on a course unless your occupation (or some other emergency situation) makes it impractical or unsafe to do so, but even if that is the case the phone should be put into silent mode. Taking an emergency call on the course is one thing, but it's bad form to carry on a phone conversation while on the course.

The main exception to the stay quiet rule is when you must alert another player of imminent danger. For example, if you hit or see a shot that looks like it may hit another golfer you should yell *'Fore!'* loud enough to be heard by the player or players in danger regardless of what else is going on.

It's also acceptable (as odd as it may seem) to yell at a ball – phrases such as 'Sit down!', 'Get legs!' and 'Hit a house!' are common phrases on the golf course (these terms are covered in the chapter on golf vocabulary). As you begin to play golf it's best if you observe others for a while before using these terms, perhaps with the exception of yelling *fore* to alert someone of an incoming ball. As you become more familiar with the subtleties of when to yell and when not to, it's best to err on the side of being quiet.

'It is expected that everyone should remain quiet while a player is hitting and putting.'

Be still

Just as important as not talking during someone's swing or putt is not moving. As you will soon be finding out, it takes a lot of concentration and precision to hit a good golf shot or make a good putt. Any distraction during the swing or follow through can cause a player to make a bad shot or miss a putt. In truth, many people make a lot of bad shots, and miss a lot of putts even if there are not people moving around. That said, it is distracting when people are moving about (especially when that movement involves walking into their line of sight or peripheral vision) while someone is swinging a club. They may have shanked it anyway so it's best not to give them someone to blame.

When someone is swinging a club, in addition to not moving around you will want to have positioned yourself outside of their field of vision. Not only does this eliminate a possible distraction but it keeps you safe as well. Even the best golfers hit errant shots and if you are in the direct line of a shot you may not have time to react. Getting hit by a golf ball can be very painful and a hard hit in a vital area can cause injury, or even death. It's rare of course, but it's always best to stay behind a golfer who is taking a swing at a ball, being sure to be far enough away so that you do not get hit by the club.

This also includes walking up behind a golfer right after they take a shot. You never know when someone may wheel around with a club or take a second swing after the ball has already travelled down the course. A good rule to follow is to stay behind the person at least two club lengths away and not approach the person who has just swung a club until they have started to walk away from their swing stance.

If you are on the fairway there will be times when you cannot get behind a golfer taking a swing. For example, you may have gone to look for your ball on one side of the fairway while your mate's shot was on the other side. You may find that you are positioned ahead of where your mate is as he prepares to hit his ball. In a case such as this it's best to try to face the person taking the swing so that you can react to an errant shot that comes towards you. Better still, if you can use a tree or cart to shield you from an errant shot.

On the putting green you cannot always get behind the person who is putting but you should be out of their putting line and be perfectly still. The main exception to this rule is if you are attending the flagstick. In this case you will lift the flagstick out of the hole in the bottom of the cup put still have the bottom of the flagstick within the cup. Be perfectly still as the person putting addresses the ball and remain still until the ball is in motion. Once the ball is in motion, lift the flagstick out of the cup and move out the way so that neither you nor the flagstick interferes with the player's ball.

Don't mess with another golfer's ball

In the previous chapter you learned that you can be assessed with a penalty for playing another person's ball on the course or for putting into another's ball on the green. As a beginner you will probably not be too worried about counting these types of penalty strokes, but you do need make sure that you don't make other golfers angry. Hitting or picking up someone else's ball is one of the biggest ways to make a golfer mad (the other way is to move or make noise while they are swinging/putting!).

A good rule to follow is this: Never touch or pick up a ball that does not belong to you unless you ask the owner of that ball of it's OK. If you can't verify whose it is, leave it alone. There of course are some exceptions. If you think the ball might be yours you can pick it up or move it slightly to verify the markings on the ball. Also, if you are looking for your ball in the woods or deep rough and you stumble upon a ball, most golfers will pick it up and keep it on the assumption that another golfer has lost it and given up looking for it. If the area you are looking in is between two holes it may have been hit there by a golfer from the other side though, so in this case it's better to leave it alone.

Making your mark

On the putting green there are some special considerations. Once all players' balls are on the green, putting begins. As mentioned in the previous chapter, the player furthest away putts first and if another player's ball is in the line of another player's putt they are expected to mark their ball and pick it up. Typically, a ball is marked with a small coin purpose-built marker. The marker is placed directly behind your ball (so that it touches the bottom of the ball). Most players place it such that the marker, ball and cup make a straight line. Once the marker is down you may pick up your ball. You are also allowed to pick up your ball to clean it (this is only allowed on the putting green under tournament rules). When it is your turn to putt simply place the ball back down in the original position and pick up the marker.

In some cases, the player who is away may be concerned that your marker may alter the trajectory of their putt (this is common when they must putt directly over the marker and there is a break in the green). If this happens you

'If another player's ball is in the line of another player's putt they are expected to mark their ball and pick it up.'

will want to offset your ball mark. It's OK to ask another player to show you how to do this the proper way. Don't be too surprised if you are not the only one who does not know how to do this.

Step out of line

There is another consideration on the green that almost everyone finds out by violating, only to be spoken to (sometimes harshly) by the player who has been affected. It is considered bad form to step in the line of another player's putt (even prior to them putting). While the odds of a foot imprint or spike mark actually altering a player's putt is very low, most players will still react negatively to someone 'stepping on their line' so it's best to avoid if possible.

Armed with this knowledge you should take a moment before marking your own ball or attending the flag to look for a route where you will not have to step on someone else's putting line in order to reach your destination on the green.

> 'It's important to repair any damage or alteration to the course that happen as a normal result of playing the game.'

Leave the course the way you found it

The beautiful course you are on did not get that way by accident and it takes a lot of work to prepare and maintain it on a daily basis. In addition to maintaining the beauty of a course (which is one of the nicest things about playing golf) it's important to repair any damage or alteration to the course that happen as a normal result of playing the game. The three areas we will focus on here are divots, sand traps and ball marks.

Repair divots

A properly swung golf club will make contact with the ball from a low position behind the ball and will follow through directly through the ball until the arc of the swing raises the club (and the ball). This swing often results in the club striking both the ground and the ball, resulting in a divot where the grass and some dirt beneath it is carved out or otherwised damaged or destroyed. When this occurs it is the golfer's responsibility to repair the damage they caused as best they can.

If there is a piece (or pieces) of turf that came out in tact, they will usually be somewhere in front of where you are standing when you hit your shot. As long as it is safe to do so, the best method for repair is to retrieve the piece(s) of turf, place it back where it was, and tamp it down lightly with your foot or a club. You may also notice plastic tubes with a pour spout near the tee box or attached to a buggy. These tubes have premixes of turf seed and starter fertiliser to promote rapid growth of grass. If this mix is available, and you cannot find the piece of turf, you should pour this mixture into the damaged area.

Smooth over sand

Another area to be mindful of when leaving the course in pristine condition is the sand traps or bunkers. While there is not normally damage that occurs in a bunker (perhaps with the exception to one's ego if you can't hit out of it), you should take extra time to rake out the bunker after you are done taking your shot(s). Near each bunker you will see a rake. After you finish your shot use the rake to rake the sand smooth where you took your shot and all your footprints. The best way to do this is to back out of the sand trap while retracing your steps. When you leave a bunker there should be no evidence that you were there. Also, remember to leave the rake to the side of the bunker – teeth down to prevent someone from getting hurt.

Keep it green

The final area of consideration is the green and it's probably the most important place to repair damage, and the trickiest thing to get right. Due to the high arcing shots that golfers tend to use on their approach, there is often an indentation left where the ball strikes the ground. If the golfer hit a high shot with a backspin these marks can be significant. However even a subtle ball mark can alter a person's putt if it's not repaired, and for the larger putts an untended ball mark can mar the green and take weeks to repair. The method for repairing a ball mark is beyond the scope of this book so it's best to look online. For example, typing in 'how to repair a ball mark' on youtube.com yields a number of videos that show how to do this properly. You can also ask the club pro to show you how (which will go a long way to impress him/her). You can also ask your mates, but be aware that many golfers (even avid golfers) get this wrong and you may be getting bad advice.

Summing Up

- Etiquette always applies, even in non-competition matches.

- While there are a lot of subtleties to the rules of golf etiquette, you can get it mostly right by first and foremost remembering to respect both the course and the other players' games.

- As with official rules – if you are unsure about something to do with golf etiquette, just ask.

Chapter Nine

The Language of Golf

Talking golf

One of the most daunting things about beginning at golf is that the game has its own language. To the uninitiated this can be a little intimidating and for some, trying to carry on a conversation with your golfing buddies may actually be as nerve-racking as standing on the first tee with everyone watching you.

Because of this specialised language we have included these terms in a full chapter rather than as a glossary, to emphasise the relevance of the language within the game

A word of advice

The two biggest mistakes most beginner golfers make with regards to using golf terms are:

- They don't ask questions about what a word or phrase means.

- They overdo it on the terms they do know.

Most golfers – at least the ones you would want to play with – will be more than happy to explain what the terms and phrases mean, and in some cases will even go out of their way to help you understand. If you hear a word or phrase that you don't know or can't remember, just ask your mate. A word of warning though; golf is a fun game and it often brings out people's mischievous side. Don't be too surprised if someone along the way makes up a bogus term to have some fun with you. If it happens, laugh it off and save it for the next new player who comes along.

The other side of this is that you don't want to overdo it on the terms. It's great when you get the hang of the language – and some terms are used more than others – but generally speaking less is more when it comes to using these terms.

A

Ace
A hole in one – this can also be used to refer to a very good golfer.

Action
The backspin on a ball which causes it to stop or roll backwards after hitting the ground.

Addressing the ball
When a golfer takes his stance and lines up the club to make a stroke.

Approach
This is both the action of the ball at the green and the area before the green.

Apron
The fringe surrounding the green.

Attend the flag
Holding and removing the flagstick from the hole as another player putts.

Away
The ball (or player) furthest from the hole. This person usually plays first.

B

Back door
When a ball is holed by going around the lip of the cup and dropping in from the back end.

Back nine
The last nine holes of an 18-hole course.

Backspin
Reverse spin onto the ball.

Backswing

The act of taking the club away from the ball – this is the first part of a golf swing.

Ball mark

The indentation left by the ball after it hits on the fairway or green.

Ball marker

Any small object used to mark a ball's position on the green.

Banana ball

This can refer to any slice, but it usually used to describe a severe slice.

Beach

A sand bunker. As in 'it landed on the beach'.

Best ball

A competition where two or more players are on a team. The best score from each team (on each hole) is used on the scorecard.

Birdie

One under par for the hole.

Bite

Refers to a ball stopping hard or rolling backwards (due to a backspin) when it hits the green. Usually a player will yell 'Bite!' after they have hit (yelling at the ball rarely works but players persist).

Blind hole

A blind hole is one where the golfer cannot see the green when having to play a shot.

Bogey

One over par for the hole.

Bogey golf

Playing a round where you average one over par per hole.

Break

The contour of a green that impacts the path of a putt.

Buggy

A motioned cart used to transport golfers around the course.

Bunker

Also referred to as a sand trap, this is a non-penalty hazard filled with sand. These are usually placed around a green but can also be on the fairway. You are not allowed to take a practice swing or set your club on the ground while addressing the ball in a bunker (this is called grounding your club).

C

Caddie

A person who carries a player's club bag. Caddies also assist a player on determining distances and club selection and determining the break of a green.

Carry

The distance that the ball travels in the air – most often used in reference to getting a ball over a hazard.

Cart path

The designated route for carts – this is usually a paved path and on many courses (especially during rainy season) the buggy must remain on the path.

Casual water

Water on the course that is not an intended water hazard (for example, large puddles after rain). You can take a free drop (or relief) from casual water without penalty.

Cavity backed

A type of iron with a hollowed out back. These clubs are easier to swing and are a good choice for beginners.

Chilli dip

Refers to an errant shot where the club comes down on the top of the ball causing it to jump straight up and come straight back down. This usually happens around the green.

Chip

A type of shot where the ball lands on the green and rolls towards the hole.

Closed face

When the position of the club face is turned slightly inward to either hook the ball (move right to left for a right-handed golfer) or prevent a slice.

Club face
The striking surface of a club.

Club loft
The angle of the club face . A high loft will increase the arc of a shot (and decrease the distance).

Cup
The hole in the green – this is the objective of each hole.

D

Dimple
The indentations on a golf a ball. When a player hits a ball especially hard or far they are said to have hit the dimples off the ball.

Divot
A piece of turf torn out when a ball is struck – typically on the fairway.

Dog-leg
A hole where the fairway turns hard to the left or right.

Double bogey
Two shots over the hole par.

Double eagle
Three shots under the hole par. This is less common than a hole in one as it requires two very long and accurate shots on a par five hole. It can also be achieved by getting a hole in one on a par 4.

Downhill lie
When the ball rests on a hill which slopes down towards the hole or the direction of your shot.

Draw
Refers to a slight movement of the ball in flight from right to left (for a right-handed golfer). This is the same motion, although less extreme than a hook. In most cases hitting a draw is considered a positive.

Drive
The first shot on a hole from the tee area.

Drop

The act of manually putting a ball back in play. The player literally holds the ball away from his/her body and drops the ball.

Duck hook

This is a severe version of a hook.

E

Eagle

A score that is two shots under par for a hole.

F

Fade

Refers to a slight motion of a ball in flight from left to right (for a right-handed golfer). Opposite of a draw, this is a less extreme version of a slice and can be considered to be a positive result when done on purpose or naturally (whereas a slice is usually a negative result of an improper swing).

Fairway

The playing area between the tee and the green. This grass is usually kept short and is easy to play from.

Fat shot

Refers to a shot where the club strikes the ground well behind the ball. A player will say 'I hit it fat'.

Flagstick

The pole with a flag attached that marks the cup.

Flex

The relative degree to which a clubs' shaft bends during the swing and impact.

Flight

A path of the ball through the air.

Follow through

This is the part of the swing after the club has struck the ball.

Fore

A loud verbal warning to alert other players that a ball may hit them. Any player (whether it's their ball or not) can yell *'Fore!'* on a course to warn players. If you hear this, cover your head.

Foursome

A group of four golfers playing together.

Fringe

The short grass (shorter than the fairway grass, but longer than the grass on the green) that surrounds the green.

G

Get down

A phrase said by golfers during their shot to convince the ball to either land or go into the hole.

Get legs

Something golfers yell to get the ball to roll further when they suspect the ball will stop short.

Gimmie

A putt that is so short that it is a virtual certainty that it will be made. In casual play the player can pick up a 'gimmie' on the assumption that they would have made it into the cup.

Green

The area of short grass surrounding the hole.

Green's fee

The costs or fees for a round of golf.

Green in regulation

Being on the green in regulation means your ball is on the green and you have two putts to make par. For a par three you must hit your first shot on the green. For a par five your third shot must land on the green to be on in regulation.

Grip

The cover on the end of a club where you hold the club while swinging. This also refers to how you hold the club (the position of the hands) during a swing.

Ground under repair

An area of the course where work is being done, or needs to be done. This is non-playable area where the ball can be removed and dropped without penalty.

Grounding the club

Placing or resting the club on the ground while addressing the ball (setting up for a shot). There are situations (such as being in a sand trap) where grounding the club results in penalty.

H

Hack or hacker

A term used to describe a bad golfer. This is usually used to describe a regular or avid golfer who is not very good as opposed to a beginner who has yet to learn how to play.

Handicap

An adjustment a player is given to their score such that on average they will be at 'par golf'. Handicaps allow golfers with different abilities to compete on equal terms.

Hazard

A permanent feature or obstacle on a golf hole designed to obstruct play.

Head

The end of the golf club.

Heel

The part of the club head attached to the shaft. To 'heel' a shot is to hit the ball with the back/top of the club rather than on the face of the club.

Hit a house

Something golfers yell at a ball when they have putted much too hard – it refers to hitting or going into the cup (thus preventing the ball from rolling past the cup).

Hole in one

Hitting the ball into the cup from the tee shot.

Hole out
Putting the ball into the hole.

Home
Refers to a ball that gets onto the green. A player will say 'get home' to a ball in flight, or will say 'I got home' when they hit the ball onto the green. Don't overuse this.

Honour
This refers to the loose rules that determine the order of play on a hole. The honour goes to the player who won the last hole, or who finished the last hole with the fewest strokes.

Hook
Refers to a shot where the ball moves from right to left in flight (for a right-handed golfer). This is the opposite of a slice and is often viewed as a flaw.

I

In play
A ball that is in bounds and playable.

Interlocking grip
To hold the club such that the little finger of one hand is wrapped around the forefinger of the other.

Iron
A club with a metal head. Usually played during fairway shots or short approaches.

K

Knockdown shot
A shot that is hit low because the player is hitting directly into the wind.

L

Lateral water hazard
A water hazard that does not require a player to hit over it to reach the green – usually a lateral water hazard runs parallel to the fairway.

Lie
The position of the ball on the ground.

Lip
The edge of the cup.

Local rules
Modifications or supplemental rules that pertain to a given course.

Loft
The angle of the clubface.

M

Match play
A form of competition where each hole is competed for. Rather than using the net score to determine a winner, the match is based on who won the most holes. In match play the player with the higher net score (which would be a loss in stroke play) could still win the match. A winning score of 3 and 2 means that the winner won by 3 holes with 2 left to play.

Mulligan
Refers to taking an extra shot on the tee box – without a penalty. In a friendly game a player will replay a bad tee shot rather than taking a penalty. If you hit a bad tee shot, you – or another player – will suggest that you 'take a mulligan'.

N

Nineteenth hole
Refers to clubhouse bar, which is often the next stop after playing 18 holes!

O

OB
Acronym for out of bounds.

Obstruction
Any man-made object that obstructs play.

On the dance floor
Refers to a ball that is on the green.

Out of bounds
The area on or adjacent to the course that is outside the playable area. Out of bounds is most often marked by white stakes.

Over par
The number of strokes over the indicated par for a hole or round. For example, on a par four a player that scored a six is said to be two over par. Scoring a 90 on a round would be 18 over par for a standard par 72 course.

P

Par
The number of shots and putts that a hole is designed to take to get from tee to hole and the total of those shots and putts for an entire course.

Penalty stroke
The number of strokes added to a player's score due to a rule infringement, or unplayable lie due to a hazard.

PGA
Professional Golfers Association.

Pin
The pole that marks the cup location on a green (also called a flagstick).

Pin high
Refers to a shot that where the ball has landed on the green level with the hole.

Pitch
A shot where the ball is hit high into the air onto the green using a lofted club.

Pitch and run
A pitch where the ball rolls on impact.

Pitching wedge
An iron with a club face angel of 48 to 50 degrees. The club will be marked with a 'P' or 'PW' on the bottom of the club head.

Playing through

The act of a faster moving player or group playing a hole while you are on the hole (in which case you and your group stand to the side) or on the tee box where a group behind you plays the next hole before you do.

Plugged ball

A ball that imbeds itself in the ground upon landing.

Pro shop

The shop or club store at golf club.

Provisional ball

The second shot that is played when a player believes that their first ball is out of bounds, in a water hazard or believed to be lost.

Putt

Act of hitting a golf ball on the green causing it to roll (rather than take flight).

Putter club

Mainly used on the green for striking the ball.

Putting green

The area of short grass surrounding the hole where the ball is hit using a putter.

Q

Quitting on the ball

The act of slowing down a swing before hitting the ball, or not following through after hitting the ball. This usually results in the ball not going as far as intended.

R

R&A

The Royal and Ancient Golf Club of St Andrew's who oversee golf in Europe and Asia.

Ranger

A course official who ensures that players keep the appropriate pace on the course.

Relief
A free drop of the ball without penalty.

Rough
The areas flanking the fairway with high grass. The ball can be played from the rough, but the longer grass makes the ball harder to hit.

Round
Playing 18 holes of golf.

Run-up
A shot where the ball remains on or close to the ground toward and onto the green.

S

Sand trap
A sand bunker.

Sand wedge
An iron with additional loft designed to get balls out of sand hazards.

Scramble
Team competition where all players play from the position of the best ball of a team member after every stroke or drive.

Scratch player
A golfer who does not require a handicap because they play par or better golf.

Shaft
The long narrow part of the club between the head and the grip.

Shank
A shot where the ball is hit with the part of the club head where the heel is joined to the shaft. This usually results in the ball careening off the club at a severe angle.

Short game
The golf shots that are made close to the hole including chipping, pitching and putting.

Shotgun start

A method of starting a tournament to reduce the total tournament time. Rather than having everyone queue up and start in turn from the first tee, each group starts on a different hole and completes the loops around the course until they have played all holes. A loud noise that can be heard throughout the course (which could be but is rarely from a shotgun) indicates that all teams should begin play.

Sit

A term players shout at their ball to encourage it to stop rolling.

Slice

A shot where the ball travels from left to right in flight for right-handed golfers (usually way to the right) due to a flaw in the swing. A slice is the opposite to a hook.

Snap hook

A severe hook.

Starter

An official who determines where and when golfers tee off.

Stroke

An attempt to hit the ball.

Summer rules

Summer rules are when the normal rules of golf apply regarding playing a ball where it lies.

Sweet spot

The spot on the club face that is the indented striking area. Hitting a ball on the sweet spot usually results in a good shot.

T

Tee

A peg stuck into the ground on which a golf ball is placed and the area golfers play their for shot from on a each hole.

Tee time

The scheduled starting time for a round of golf.

Tempo
The speed of a golf swing.

Temporary green
A green that is used when the normal green is under repair or off limits due to other conditions.

Tending the flag
Holding the flagstick while another player lines up and putts the ball. The flag is removed from the cup once the ball is in motion.

Tight fairway
A narrow fairway.

Top
To hit or strike the ball above the mid point. This usually results in the ball popping up or bouncing along the ground rather than flying through the air.

Trouble shot
A shot hit from a really bad lie or from the deep rough or behind on object (such as a tree).

Turn
The midway point on a golf course, usually the 9th hole (on some courses play can start on the tenth hole rather than the first hole). 'Making the turn' refers to starting the second half of the round.

W

Waggle
Movement of the club head at the beginning or the top of a swing.

Water hazard
Any pond, lake, river or other permanent water on a course. Water hazards are marked by yellow or red stakes.

Wedge
An iron designed to hit a high, but relatively short shot. Most often used around the green.

Whiff
To swing and miss at the ball.

Winter rules

Local rules which among other things allow a player to improve their lie by moving the ball without a penalty.

Worm burner

A shot which stays low to the ground.

Y

Yips

To miss short putts due to nerves. This usually happens when money is on the line.

Help List

Golf resources (UK)

British Golf Museum

www.britishgolfmuseum.co.uk/
Site dedicated to the world's premier golf heritage centre, at the old course at St Andrews.

Classic Heritage Golf Tours

www.golfresource.com/england/
Classic Heritage Golf Tours plans and manages luxury golf travel for groups.

Direct Golf UK

www.direct-golf.co.uk
One of the largest specialist golf retailers in the UK and Europe.

England Golf

www.englandgolf.org/
Site for the governing body of amateur golf in England.

English Golf Courses

www.englishgolf-courses.co.uk
Offers a comprehensive listing of every single golf course in England.

Fine Golf

www.finegolf.co.uk/
Discover the finest golf courses with the 'joy to be alive' factor. A passionate campaign for golf's classic values.

Golfalot

www.golfalot.com/
Golf equipment and golf course reviews.

Golf Monthly

www.golf-monthly.co.uk/
Golf tips and expert instruction – includes a guide to the UK and Ireland's golf courses.

Golfonline

www.golfonline.co.uk/
Online golf shop for equipment, clubs, shoes, bags and balls.

Golf School UK

www.golfschool.co.uk/
Golf website links and resources for beginners and low handicap golfers.

Golf Today

www.golftoday.co.uk/clubhouse/coursedir/england.html
English golf course listing,

Onlinegolf,

www.onlinegolf.co.uk/
One of Europe's largest golf shops – large range of golf equipment, golf clubs, golf clothing, and golf shoes at web only prices.

Planet Golf UK

www.planetgolfuk.co.uk
Offers low cost golf equipment and accessories from a wide range of products from leading manufacturers.

Rate Your Course UK

www.rateyourcourse.co.uk/
A good golf resource where visitors can search for golf courses, book a hotel or rate a course.

Today's Golfer

www.todaysgolfer.co.uk/
A site dedicated to helping readers and visitors play better, buy better and choose the best places to play.

Top 100 Golf Courses

www.top100golfcourses.co.uk/
Listing of the top golf courses in the UK.

UK Golf Directory

www.uk-golfdirectory.co.uk
Large list of UK golf sites in a directory format

UK Golf Guide

www.ukgolfguide.com
Listing of every golf course in the UK along with up-to-date contact details, scorecards, course information, photos, reviews, local information and tee times.

UK Golf Society

www.golfsocieties.uk.net/
A course listing for the UK and Ireland's golf societies.

Urban Golf

www.urbangolf.co.uk/
Site for London-based golf facility with three indoor golf venues using state-of-the-art golf simulators. Play 52 championship golf courses, or improve with golf lessons from experts.

Where2Golf.com

www.where2golf.com
An online guide to the UK, Ireland, Scotland courses.

Golf resources (Ireland)

Golf.com

www.golf.com/special-features/18-best-courses-ireland
The 18 best golf courses in Ireland according to GOLF.com.

Golfing Ireland

www.golfinginireland.ie/
Offers golf holidays, links, courses, tours and vacation accommodation packages.

Golfing Union of Ireland

www.gui.ie
The oldest golfing union in the world.

Ireland Golf Resources

www.ireland-fun-facts.com/ireland-golf-resources.html
A list of useful links for planning a golf trip to Ireland.

Irish Golf Courses

www.irishgolfcourses.co.uk/
The Internet home of Irish golf.

Online Golf Travel

www.onlinegolftravel.com/ireland/golf-in-ireland/
Book golf courses in Ireland – tee times and Ireland golf travel

Ritson-Sole Golf Schools

www.ritson-sole.com/golf/
Established golf directory designed to help golfers find quality online resources for golfing in Ireland.

The Golfer's Guide To Ireland

www.golfersguide.ie/
An interactive version of the 'The Golfers Guide To Ireland'.

Wild Kerry Day Tours

www.wildkerry-daytours.ie/ireland_tour_golf.html
Guided golf tours of Ireland

Golf resources (Scotland)

Green Fee Savers

www.greenfeesavers.co.uk/golf-instruction.html
Guide to Scottish and UK golf instructors

Golf Scotland

www.golfscotland.com/
Golf Scotland specialises in Scottish golf vacations and luxury golf tours and
VIP golf.

Olde Scotland Links

www.oldescotlandlinks.com/
Online guide for premiere golfing in Scotland

Scotland for Golf

www.scotlandforgolf.co.uk/
Scotland for Golf offer a wide range of luxury, bespoke golfing trips, tours and
vacation packages.

Scotland Golf

www.scotlandgolf.com/
Comprehensive listing and reservation site for Scottish golf.

Scottish Golf Courses

www.scottishgolfcourses.com/
A guide to all of Scotland's golf courses detailed by region.

Scottish Golf Show

www.thescottishgolfshow.co.uk/professionaltuition.html
Information on the Scottish Golf Show where they are offering free lessons for players of all standards available from fully-qualified PGA pros.

WorldGolf.com

www.worldgolf.com/courses/scotland/
A guide to all of Scotland's golf courses detailed by region plus course reviews, golf packages, articles and reference pages.

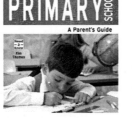

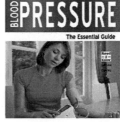